HOLIDAYS ON DISPLAY

holidays on display

WILLIAM L. BIRD, JR.

SMITHSONIAN INSTITUTION, NATIONAL MUSEUM OF AMERICAN HISTORY, WASHINGTON, D.C.,

IN ASSOCIATION WITH PRINCETON ARCHITECTURAL PRESS, NEW YORK

HALF-TITLE ART Framed silhouette "greeting card" displayed on the grounds of Nela Park, General Electric Company's lighting research campus, Cleveland, Ohio, 1953

PUBLISHED BY
Princeton Architectural Press
37 East Seventh Street
New York, New York 10003

For a free catalog of books, call 1.800.722.6657.
Visit our web site at www.papress.com.

EDITOR: Jennifer N. Thompson
DESIGNER: Sara E. Stemen

SPECIAL THANKS TO: Nettie Aljian, Sara Bader, Dorothy Ball, Nicola Bednarek, Janet Behning, Becca Casbon, Penny (Yuen Pik) Chu, Russell Fernandez, Pete Fitzpatrick, Wendy Fuller, Jan Haux, Clare Jacobson, John King, Nancy Eklund Later, Linda Lee, Katharine Myers, Lauren Nelson Packard, Paul Wagner, Joseph Weston, and Deb Wood of Princeton Architectural Press

—Kevin C. Lippert, publisher

LIBRARY OF CONGRESS CATALOGING-IN-PUBLICATION DATA
Bird, William L.
  Holidays on display / William L. Bird, Jr. — 1st ed.
      p. cm.
  Includes bibliographical references.
  ISBN-13: 978-1-56898-695-1 (alk. paper)
  ISBN-10: 1-56898-695-5 (alk. paper)
  1. Show windows—United States—History.
  2. Christmas show windows—United States—History.
  3. Holiday decorations—United States—History.
  I. National Museum of American History (U.S.) II. Title.
  HF5845.B444 2006
  659.1'57—dc22
                                                    2007004344

CONTENTS

SCALE 1" PER 1"

FRANCIS SCOTT KEY

INTRODUCTION : CREATING THE HOLIDAY SPIRIT

THIS BOOK IS FOR THOSE of a certain age with a memory of a fleeting retail landscape on the cusp of suburban expansion in the late 1950s and early 1960s, a landscape that, having reached the point of retail saturation, is vastly different today—characterized by the decline of city centers, the Spartan appearance of big box retailers, and the middle ground of the shopping mall. It is not the author's intent to catalog or to describe all of holiday display, even if that were possible. Rather it is to describe the art and industry of display from the point of view of the artists, producers and clients for whom holidays—especially Christmas—maximized the possibilities of creative self-expression.

A metaphor in the largest sense of the word, *Holidays on Display* explores the history of display's most emotionally successful visual elements: outdoor lighting, animated windows, and parade floats. I have chosen to describe these as the amenities of what one found while walking around town. Though commercially inspired, these amenities created emotional bonds between their sponsors and the public that transcended commercial meaning.

Historians typically cite the made-up aspects of holiday traditions to emphasize the social and political uses to which they have been put.[1] If and when display is discussed as *display*,

1

little consideration is given to its emotional impact, although that is arguably the basis of its memorable effect. More easily felt than measured, an emotional effect began with something interesting to look at. In weighing the development of modern display and its popular appeal, the historiography of American pageantry perhaps comes closest to this truth, followed by the historiography of the democratic values and visual strategies shared by museums and department stores.[2]

The realization of emotional effects in lighting, animation, and miniaturization followed the display world's newest responsibilities from window to street. Many trimmers built their decorative livelihoods from scratch with readily available materials such as natural flowers and evergreen coverings, crepe paper, papier-mâché, electric motors, and socket sets. The will-to-create cut across class lines and social strata. Lamping engineers, for example, created elaborate outdoor Christmas displays. While such displays were initially justified as business expenses, they had more to do with the creative energy that made a medium out of what was thought to be a utilitarian, industrial product. In a similar fashion, papier-mâché sculptors of animal and human figures discovered small electrical motors, creating a new animated entertainment that won comment and attention as a holiday attraction. The machine was the least of it. Many of the same artists created artificial floral sheeting from colored crepe and tissue paper and applied it to hay wagons, trucks, trailers, and automobiles, the point being to suspend disbelief while the underlying vehicle floated down the street in the line of march.

In an era in which the cinema and the amusement park were still in a nascent stage of development, holiday display provided a creative outlet for its builders, a competitive attraction for its sponsors, and entertainment value for its audience. Throughout the twentieth century, new techniques of entertainment and ingratiation created a tangible connection between this audience and its sponsors who made their livelihood in the lively downtown. Between 1900 and 1920 display latched onto every mechanical and electrical feature and device that could be adapted for an emotional effect. An elaborate projection, of sorts, the effect shaped ideas about community and prosperity, focused most intensively in the urban retail core.

The department store represented the single largest market for display, and here specialists expended their greatest efforts in fulfilling the objectives of a free show. Attitudes about art and its relationship to the store were changing, along with the influx of professionally trained graduates of college and museum art programs. Populating the in-house display studios of major department stores, many enjoyed nearly unrestricted influence in the appearance of their stores, which were characterized by local owners who took pride in the competitive advantages of display and spent accordingly. Their holiday displays resonate today in the traditions of decorative lighting, animated windows, and parades that make the visual announcement of Christmas.

This book is for anyone who has ever seen a holiday display and wondered about where it came from, who created it, and where it went.

Petal
No. 1

Sweet Pea
Inside Petal
No. 4

Sweet Pea
Outside Petal
No. 5

Morning Glory
Petal
No. 21

Calyx
No. 2

Sweet Pea
Leaf
No. 3

Jonquil
Center Tube
No. 6

Sheath
No. 8

Hollyhock
(5 Petals)
No. 17

Calyx
No. 22
Morning Glory

Hollyhock Bud Calyx
No. 18

Hollyhock
Small Leaf
No. 19

Hollyhock
Leaf
No. 20

Pond Lily
Leaf
No. 26

Wisteria
Petals
No. 33

Rose
Calyx
No. 63

Wisteria
Petals
No. 35

Poinsettia
Leaf
No. 44

Wired
Poinsettia
Petal
Large Size
No. 43

Wired
Poinsettia
Petal
Medium Size
No. 42

Unwired
Poinsettia
Petal
Medium Size
No. 46

(7) Inches)

Unwired
Poinsettia
Petals
Large Size
No. 47

(13 Inches)

Cellophane Flower
Petal
No. 64

Wisteria
Petals
No. 34

Published by
Dennison Manufacturing
Framingham, Mass. U. S. A.

OPPOSITE FOREGROUND Automobile decorated with roses, streamers, and butterflies made of floral tissue, *Art & Decoration*, Dennison's, 1914 BACKGROUND Crepe paper and cellophane flower templates, 1929

CHAPTER 1 : DISPLAY WORLD

AT THE TURN OF THE TWENTIETH CENTURY, the occupation of window trimming—soon to be known as display—acknowledged a new and growing responsibility: the decorative appearance of the shopping holiday. To create a festive atmosphere from the store to the street, trimmers took their visual cues from popular forms of celebration and commemoration. Among their lasting contributions to culture was a popular and technically accomplished vocabulary of dimensional display that conflated public life and personal meaning. As a consequence, many Americans developed lasting emotional attachments to stores—specifically, their animated holiday windows and themed interior displays, the parades they sponsored, and the ambient glow of the walking around town that persisted in memory even after the stores themselves moved on or ceased to exist.

Trimmers welcomed the annual coming of Christmas as the ultimate season for creative display. The holiday season worked to professional advantage where budgets were fat and effects most heartfelt, and that was found most everywhere. For example, in 1894 Harry Harman, an "artistic decorator and window draper" from Louisville, Kentucky, noted the "jostling multitude"

The trimmer's tools and draping techniques for window displays, *A Textbook on Mercantile Decoration*, 1903

of sightseers that filled the streets "in front of the most attractive window and the building decorated and illuminated." Harman published a mail-order display supply catalog filled with imaginative treatments for sales floors and building exteriors, including windows. This was something new and to be argued for. "What better advertisement does a Merchant want? And what are the results?" asked Harman. "The crowd, dazzled by the grand effect, will enter the store, and purchase, whereas, if your store was not made attractive, the crowd of people would pass by." Like his peers, Harman placed special emphasis upon show windows. *Santa Claus in a "Snowstorm"*, *Santa Claus Coming Down the Chimney*, *Arrangement of Dolls*, *Winter Scenes*, and *A Stalactite Cave* featured white cotton cloth tacked to window ceilings, floors, and side walls. Irregularly arranged wooden boxes draped with cotton sheeting pinned with batting formed mountainous backdrops dusted with white flour and the frosty flitter of diamond dust.[1]

In the hands of the budding trade's clever promoters, the popularity of the holiday show window justified the utility of all windows. The *Show Window* magazine, edited by L. Frank Baum (soon celebrated for his *Wizard of Oz* children's stories), noted that Christmas raised the bar of expectation for displays that set new standards for consumer attraction. "The recent holiday displays," Baum editorialized in 1899, "have thoroughly demonstrated the progress of the art of window trimming. Every village and hamlet in the land has had some sort of a window display of unusual

merit to attract the public and further the sale of Christmas wares."[2] Baum never tired of noting that colorful décor reaped sales, and never more so than at holiday time. Retail specialists calculated that the value of merchandise sold in November and December equaled that sold in all other months combined. With that economic justification the "merchant's duty" became clear. No "false economy" would turn back expenditures for holiday display on an "elaborate scale."[3]

So popular had display become that the *Dry Goods Economist*'s Frank L. Carr, Jr., claimed for trimmers a measure of responsibility for the "architectural renaissance" of the city center, glazed over with "the all-popular and prevailing plate glass." Carr noted however, that the torrid pace of construction had overtaken the training of competent trimmers. "The field is ample," he concluded, "but the really skilled laborers are few."[4] The position demanded the carpentry skills needed to square a frame, the artistic temperament to drape a fixture, and the business sense to make it pay. Describing the qualities of the ideal trimmer, Baum and his editorial descendants imagined go-getters like themselves, possessing business minds with a flair for the artistic. When they pictured their method they spoke uncritically of "business art," as if the interests of business and art were one and the same.[5]

Display employment ranged from trimming to sign painting and show card writing, and these touched upon established retail occupations in sales, advertising, and accounting. It is worth

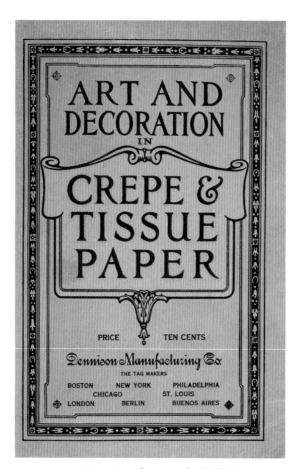

ABOVE AND OPPOSITE Manufacturers of colorful tissue papers offered a practical alternative to floats decorated with cut flowers.

noting the sweep of attention claimed for the trimmer's business-art and its application beyond the window. Jerome A. Koerber of Philadelphia's Strawbridge & Clothier, for example, encouraged trimmers to take advantage of "after hours" opportunities, urging every trimmer to develop a system of contacts to gather "regular and occasional business" such as weddings, balls, banquets, and parties.[6] Baum's Show Window paid close attention to the promotional opportunities of the street fair and the parades of flower-decked floats that were popular in the early 1900s. Baum encouraged trimmers to solicit contracts and sponsorships for the construction of kiosks and floats that called for the same construction techniques used for window treatments.[7] The extension of trimming from window to street was as much an exercise in professional advancement as an effort to stimulate popular demand for colorful décor for social and public occasions. Parades brought crowds to town, made business for merchants and "easy money" for float-building trimmers. The parade's main effect, however, gained recognition for the trimmers.[8]

Though not usually thought of together today, the show window and the parade float were very much of a piece. Windows and floats shared common materials and construction techniques and could be accomplished with materials from the local lumber yard and the specialized crepe and tissue paper supply houses sprouting up in Illinois and New York. The producers of display props aggressively moved into the production of floral tissue that replaced flowers. These firms

THE NEW DENNISON CREPE

For many years Dennison Crepe has been the standard paper decorative material the world over. Now its famous qualities have been still further improved. It is 32% *stronger*. It has a correct range of 48 colors which supply artistic and practical combinations in almost endless variety. The shades of each color group also blend one with the other in beautiful harmony. Added strength and added beauty make the New Dennison Crepe more workable, more durable, more versatile — more satisfactory in every way for craft and decorative uses.

Dennison Crepe has many qualities that make it the choice of the flower-maker, the craft-worker, and the decorator. It is finely creped and has a lovely, lustrous surface, soft and velvety on one side, satin-like on the other. Its texture, strong and yet very elastic, permits easy manipulation. These features, together with the wide variety of beautiful blending colors in which it is made, render Dennison Crepe a favorite material for flowers, costumes, favors, table decorations, curtains, novelties and window decorations.

The New Dennison Crepe is stocked in 48 beautiful shades and colors. This new and correct color scale, approved by the artist and the decorator, provides a blending range of shades in every color.

Each fold of Dennison Crepe is packaged in a new individual container which insures the material reaching the consumer in perfect condition. A carton of a dozen folds of Dennison Crepe weighs about 3¾ pounds. The shipping weight of Dennison Crepe in gross lots, packed in a fibre case is about 45 pounds.

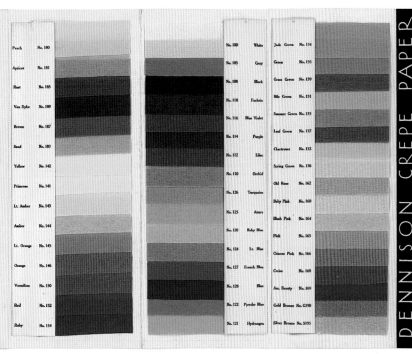

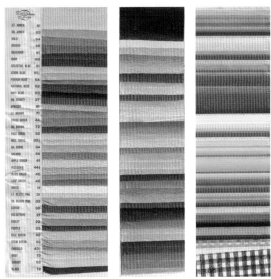

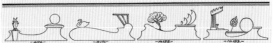

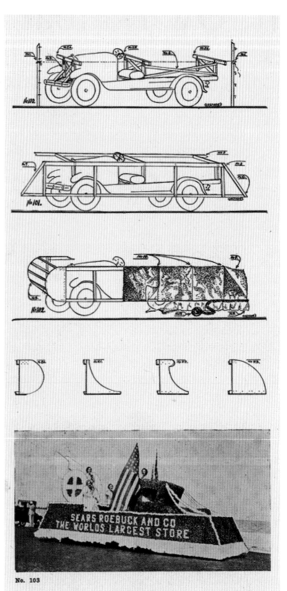

Gasthoff's parade float catalog, 1938. Floral tissue manufacturer John Gasthoff marketed the first parade float kits in 1911. Tacked to a wooden framework typically built over an automobile, floral tissue and fringe indulged the fantasy of a "float" that concealed the vehicle's operating features.

published elaborate supply catalogs of patented tissue papers, garlands, and float designs. John F. Gasthoff, for example, encouraged trimmers to enclose float designs with their supply orders, which would be returned as a kit with the components to decorate a proper float. Gasthoff's ads pictured his company's floral tissue creations in a far-flung parade circuit stretching from the company's home office in Danville, Illinois, to Texas and Florida.[9] Chicago's Joseph Schack, a rival patent holder and manufacturer of floral sheeting products, explained the logic of it all: "the Floral Parade is of benefit to both—a business getter to the merchant, a moneymaker to the decorator."[10]

Much as Baum and others anticipated, the decorative method of window display was readily extended to parades. Typically, float construction developed as a lucrative sideline among trimmers who engaged in piece work for national advertisers of liquor, cigarettes, and coffee. Often float construction became the most satisfying part of a trimmer's occupational life. Display man Earl Hargrove, for example, recalled his start in his father's display service in the 1930s, trimming liquor store windows. By the 1960s, Hargrove's display business included a thriving float-building circuit radiating from Washington, D.C.; north to Atlantic City, New Jersey; and south to Shreveport, Louisiana. Display man Lynn Smith recalled the modest origin of his father's Fargo, North Dakota, display service, "pulling crepe" for package goods stores and the itinerant trimming jobs—dance halls mostly—that financed his parents' honeymoon after the repeal

Parade float catalog, 1930. Chicago Artificial Flower developed a lucrative line of prize-winning float kits with decorations first created for window displays.

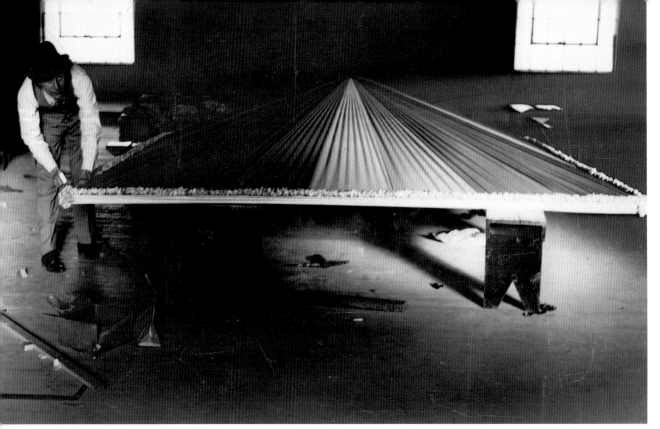

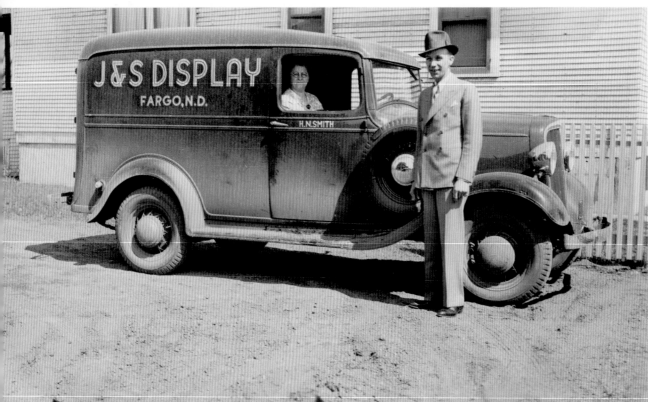

of Prohibition. Buoyed by dance halls and 3.2 beer, Smith's trimming business took off in a flurry of crepe and floral sheeting. By 1950 his father had become completely dedicated to float construction, serving clients from Fargo to Kansas City, Missouri, and Minneapolis, Minnesota.[11]

The most emotionally successful elements of display evolved from a compulsion to create. Making "business art," however, was complicated by the unsettled question of display's relationship to traditional advertising. While once it may have been sufficient for a trimmer to act the artist in a business situation, the hard-nosed realities of the business world suggested otherwise. A. E. Hurst of New York's Economist Training School, for example, warned trimmers away from those who would "place you in the same class with long-haired artists." Hurst suggested that trimmers "supplement the now too common expression show window art with show window *advertising*."[12]

Buffeted by the claims of print advertising (whose champions seemed to win a larger portion of a store's budget that might have been shared with display), the trimmer could take comfort that scientific investigation revealed that consumers gained their "strongest impressions from sight." Industry observers noted that the movies had hastened this welcome development among "eye-minded" consumers, a boon for displays that carried out "the picture idea for the store."[13] Julius Schneider, the advertising director of the *Chicago Herald*, noted that the window's "potency" was "recognized almost unconsciously." Schneider cited

the paper's masthead that claimed, somewhat ironically, to be "Chicago's Show Window."[14]

As display specialists struggled to extend their influence into the frame of paid space, the proponents of "business art" found a voice in professional organizations that abandoned "trimmer" and "dresser" as occupational descriptors. In their place they adopted "display man," an expression better suited for the elevation of their artistic method to a reliable generator of sales.[15]

The idea that display could be taught as a system took hold in the merchandising of vocational education. Chicago's Koester School, for example, offered instruction in retail advertising, show card writing, scenic painting, and modern art decorative painting. The school pictured the graduate trimmer ascending the stairway to success like a Horatio Alger hero. Though school literature included salutations to the occasional female student, more typically it emphasized the up-from-the-bootstraps success awaiting the retail clerk who studied to become a window display man. While the Koester School vouched for graduates' "artistic ability," it took pains to note that student prospects of comparable ability would likely remain clerks for lack of its system of instruction, forever cut off from the opportunities awaiting the graduate display man. Display offered exposure throughout the store among a range of contacts from buyers to admen to department managers, thus multiplying the chances for advancement. Even for students starting near the bottom of the field, the rewards for creative endeavor seemed limitless.[16]

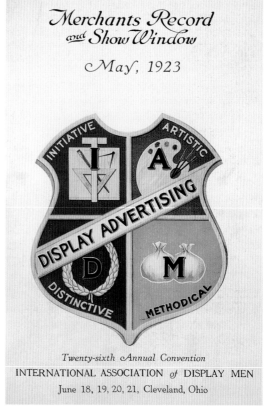

ABOVE Cartoon, *The Koester School Yearbook*, Chicago, 1913. In its own methodical way, trade school literature pictured the graduate trimmer ascending a stairway to success.

RIGHT The ambitions of "display men" could be read in the logo of the IADM, whose professional goals included the elevation of the decorative art of the "trimmer" to that of a profession.

A faith in literal display buoyed the establish-ment of store display departments, abetted by a service corps of outside contract artists, illustrators, and designers. The contracting of work held certain advantages for the stores. The New York commercial artist Harry Taylor, for example, advertised his eagerness to build "decorative sets, screens—column decorations, single cut-outs, or entire villages." Leaving no decorative stone unturned, Taylor promised "any subjects of all times, places, or countries" including "Mother Goose—Fairy Tales—Old English Colonial, or whatever you say."[17]

With few exceptions, the credit for success accrued to the display manager. Contractors carefully avoided taking public responsibility for ideas. Albert Bliss of New York's Bliss Display Corporation, a wildly successful display firm that created animated Christmas window display sets for Lord & Taylor, Macy's, and Altman's, attributed his success to his clients' ideas. "Every good idea we ever had originated with our customers," Bliss modestly proclaimed.[18] Some display artists chafed under the unwritten rule that disallowed public credit for privately contracted work. The commercial display artist Landy R. Hales, for example, took exception when Macy's display manager Irving Eldridge received public credit for a 1933 Christmas window set that Hales had suggested. Hales's idea let the window audience enjoy a view of child manikins in a railroad passenger car cutaway, while a panoramic scrim of miniature animated figures representing Christmas customs in foreign lands looped past the car's windows. Contention

New York's Harry Taylor advertised his studio's services in storybook style. Independent commercial artists and designers became important in filling the seasonal display needs of stores.

OPPOSITE Landy R. Hales's studio, Princess Theater, West 49th Street, New York, ca. 1923. Hales's display studio devised advertising displays and stage props for Morris Gest's *Parade of the Wooden Soldiers*. Hales is seated at the table, left of center.

ABOVE AND OVERLEAF Hales's animated window set, *Around the World at Christmas Time*, Macy's 34th Street, 1933

rarely made it into print. Hales noted his in the margin of a scrapbook pasted with a newspaper account of Macy's "famous moving windows," "as colorful and unusual as they've ever been before." With predictable effect Hales's finished tableaux transported the reviewer back nearly sixty years to the "epoch-making" days of Macy's Fourteenth Street window.[19]

Individual trimmers and display men forever argued about the rules and responsibilities of professional conduct. Whereas display's turn-of-the-century practitioners sought qualities that arrested attention, a new generation of specialists developed an appreciation for the irrational art of persuasion. The creation of memorable emotional appeal—what made passersby stop, why they looked, and what made them shoppers—was a job that display was uniquely qualified to do. The strength of display was its special claim upon the imagination, at once artistic, elusive, and unchartable. Holiday display offered the trimmer his most creative opportunity and in this instance was welcomed as a gift by trimmer and public alike.

CHAPTER 2 : MECHANICAL, ELECTRICAL, AND EMOTIONAL EFFECTS

BY 1900 IT WAS POSSIBLE for Americans to be nostalgic about holiday display in the nation's urban centers. As early as 1870 commercial reports noticed the cheering effect of merchants' annual preparations for Christmas, "the reminiscence of the season that changes the sentiments of men, a something that thaws out hearts."[1] In New York that something ran along Fourteenth Street up Sixth Avenue from Macy's to Lord & Taylor at Twenty-third Street, and in the Astor Place neighborhood of the former Alexander T. Stewart store at Eighth Street and Broadway that was taken over by John Wanamaker in 1896. The displays most often commented upon featured toys.[2]

By the 1880s department store window displays began to be mechanized in rudimentary ways, powered by spring mechanisms, steam, and eventually electrical power. A common display strategy integrated toy merchandise with animated figures, static figures mounted to a moving track, or both in a "mechanical panoply tableau." In 1901 *Show Window* noted that the "mechanical panoply tableau idea" had played so often in Macy's Fourteenth Street window that it had become

Eden Musée trade card, 1885. The artists of the popular wax museum created animated window displays for Macy's.

Macy's Christmas window, *Frank Leslie's Illustrated Newspaper*, 1884. Macy's "mechanical panoply tableau" featured a circular parade of figures and triumphal cars revolving on a track in the window.

NEW YORK CITY.—A HOLIDAY SPECTACLE— THE SHOW WINDOW OF MACY & CO., CORNER OF SIXTH AVENUE AND FOURTEENTH STREET. FROM A SKETCH BY A STAFF ARTIST.—SEE PAGE 254.

"part and parcel" of the store's business. That year's window featured a "Red Star Circus" of animated riders, clowns, jugglers, and acrobats. Additional scenes included "children hanging up their stockings, Santa filling them while they sleep, and so forth." *Show Window*'s appreciative reviewer noted that "It is just the old story treated in the old way, but to the children it is ever new and ever delightful." Macy's tableau compared favorably to the "Dream of Santa Claus" set in the great rotunda of Wanamaker's at Astor Place. "Were it not for the great similarity in these shows from year to year they would probably be voted the greatest hit in New York."[3]

In the pre-cinema world of New York those hits included the theater, the electrical signs of Times Square, the wax museum, and the seasonal attractions of Coney Island. Based upon the premise that what moved was more interesting than what stood still, the clockwork universe of automata was highly regarded for its commercial potential. Anecdotal evidence includes the appearance of a mechanical singing bird that R. H. Macy purchased early in the store's history dating to 1858. The bird sang to Macy friend P. T. Barnum, who came to Fourteenth Street to see it, less with wonder than pecuniary envy. Macy displayed the bird as a curiosity, not a sale item, furthering the idea that a department store might compete as a popular destination with Barnum's American Museum, or in later years, the Eden Musée whose artists created lifelike wax figures for the store's annual Christmas tableau.[4]

While creators of automata strove to create mechanical figures that looked more than mechanical, the mania for animated figures drove department stores to exhibit actors who simulated the robotic movements of machines. Actors appearing in Chicago department store windows, for example, included a "moving wax man" and a "charming old lady busy at her spinning wheel" who "doesn't seem to be the real thing that she is."[5] Many more department stores, however, warmed to the toy-like quality of mechanical figures much as Macy and Barnum did, believing that charming effects counted for more than a mastery of mechanics.[6]

In what may be the earliest reported use of an animated window by a New York City department store, Ehrich Brothers mounted a three-ring "Dolls' Circus" in 1881. The show occupied a single show window (seventeen feet wide by twenty-eight feet deep) at Eighteenth Street and Sixth Avenue. A

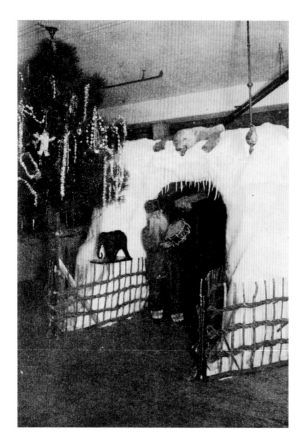

Santa Claus grotto by Leonard Shogrun for Emery, Bird, Thayer Dry Goods Co., Kansas City, Missouri, 1899

miniature parade played under a canvas big top before an audience of five thousand dolls "of all stations in doll-life" seated "tier above tier" on three sides of a sawdust-covered arena. The night before the show opened, a crowd of youthful spectators peeked at the circus around the edge of a curtain drawn over the window, reacting like the doll spectators that continuously "gaze[d] upon the performance with unmitigated surprise."[7]

Historian Ralph M. Hower cites 1883 as the year that Macy's first presented a window with moving figures animated by steam power, perhaps diverted from the store's heating system. The following year *Leslie's Illustrated* pictured a comparable parade tableau in the store's Fourteenth Street window, in which human-scale figures appear to be taking a trip on a panoramic track led by Santa in a triumphal car.[8] Macy attempted to sell these Christmas displays to out-of-town stores after their first use in New York. After-market sales recouped some of the cost of mounting increasingly ambitious holiday spectacles and set the pace for the diffusion of innovative display ideas throughout the country.[9]

The animated display field remained a novelty well into the first decades of the new century. Trimmers were beset by the mechanics of animation and a business philosophy that had only recently come to terms with the show window's value as an advertising medium. Baum's *Show Window* magazine regularly awarded prizes for meritorious displays, and it was Baum who sheepishly noted that most of his magazine's awards had gone to animated windows made by mechanically minded hobbyists who happened to have become trimmers. In 1899 Baum recommended the animated displays of Leonard Shogran, a young trimmer at Emery, Bird, Thayer Dry Goods Company of Kansas City, Missouri. Shogran specialized in miniature fire effects for model volcanoes, blacksmith forges, and Christmas tableaux. Baum's eye for talent extended to Shogran's Santa Claus "grotto," a special display space set aside for children's visits to Santa in the upper reaches of the store to pull visitors "all through the array of tempting stock." Baum also cited the "beautiful and elaborate" grotto work of display manager Charles W. Morton of Sacramento, California's, Weinstock-Lubin & Company, noting the naturalistic representation of icicles, wreaths of evergreens, Santa masks, and two fully trimmed revolving Christmas trees.[10] Baum justified his awards by observing passersby and their apparent emotional connection to mechanical effects. "It's the old idea of first catching your hare and then cooking it," Baum explained. "But you must catch your hare. You must have an attraction that induces the pedestrian to stop and look, or your window is a flat failure. That is why beautiful, artistic, and mechanical displays are to be encouraged rather than discouraged. These are real 'business windows.'"[11]

Though grottoes were largely replaced by Santalands and Tudor towns in the first decades of the twentieth century, the theme was periodically revived. In 1920, for example, Macy's staged its Santa "in a little toy cave where it was the youngsters' delight to discover him." At Selfridge's London in 1930, children and parents snaked through a half-mile queue to visit the *Headquarters of Father Christmas and His Treasure Caves.* Participating in an early form of well-themed line maintenance, visitors negotiated a baffle route of "subterraneous caverns and grottoes" with "floral growths" and "curious sea monsters" backlit by tanks of subtropical fish. One exhausted but satisfied visitor noted that "it was a struggle to pass on as quick as the pressing crowds compel one to do, for the desire is very strong to linger and enjoy the tableaux more fully."[12]

The idea that there could be no greater attraction than a themed display transformed the department store. Animation resonated with merchants who conceived the store as an amenity-filled machine for selling and who keenly integrated its operation with the social life of the walking around town. An "open" or "exposition-style" scheme characterized the display of merchandise in functional categories that pleased, invited, and overwhelmed.[13]

Display's growing importance as an institutional manner of speaking at holiday time coincided with the end of the age of store building. The nation's largest retailers finished constructing flagship stores in New York, Philadelphia, and Chicago by the 1910s, and in the mid-1920s settled into strategies of competitive visual presentation to distinguish themselves.[14] The most exceptional acknowledgment of display's arrival as an advertising medium were the "elevator windows" of Lord & Taylor's new Fifth Avenue building. Each window platform on the Fifth Avenue storefront

Seigel, Cooper Co., Chicago, 1909. Display capitalized upon enormous expanses of plate glass to project a festive atmosphere from building to street.

was elevated by a hydraulic lift from the basement and sub-basement. Working out of sight, trimmers used a trolley system to change window platforms that could now be modeled in advance and raised into place at street level as needed.[15] Along State Street in Chicago, the completion of Marshall Field & Company in 1902 anchored rival plate glass behemoths to the south—Carson Pirie Scott & Company, Siegel-Cooper & Company, the Boston Store, and The Fair—while in Philadelphia, the building for John Wanamaker's "new kind of store" completed in 1910 anchored mercantile expansion on Market Street including Strawbridge & Clothier, Gimbels, and Lit Brothers.[16]

Allusions to classical forms such as triumphal arches, cars, and cornucopia completed the picture of the holiday store. For example, an illustrated children's booklet given as a souvenir of a visit to Santa by the Kresge Department Store of Newark, New Jersey, pictured a towering store building groaning with a surfeit of toys that threaten to cascade from the roof at any moment. Evergreen trees trim the store's exterior seen through a fence with an open gate under an arch. A figure of Santa beckons.[17] Marshall Field & Company distributed a paper novelty "treasure chest" to get shoppers up to Field's fourth-floor toy department. This children's souvenir opened to reveal paper cutouts of toy merchandise and an equally graphic representation of Field's State Street building. An enclosed map of Chicago pictured the store as a multistory treasure chest occupying a city block.[18]

While trying to differentiate their stores from others, display men and managers settled, almost universally, for familiar childhood themes drawn from the circus. Until they were displaced by animated papier-mâché figures, live circus acts dominated holiday entertainment in Chicago and New York in the 1910s. The trade press noted a veritable arms race among Chicago stores to present circus scenes on an elaborate scale. Siegel-Cooper & Company filled a solid block of its State Street frontage with mechanical window tableaux and, inside on the fourth floor, an exhibition of wild animals. This exhibit totaled some eighteen thousand square feet featuring a walk-through jungle of live trees, shrubbery and artificial rocks, and a one-ring circus with professional performers, including clowns, acrobats, performing dogs, ponies, and other animals in a continuous show. An

Paper novelty toy chest, Marshall Field & Co., 1925. In an attempt to get street side shoppers to its fourth floor toy department, Marshall Field presented its State Street store as a treasure chest that contained paper cut-outs of the building and miniature merchandise.

orchestra furnished light music. Down the street, the Fair exhibited a traveling menagerie-type circus show. Animals in cages lined the store interior for the length of the block. Apparently having failed to engage an off-season circus, the Boston Store exhibited the "Marvelous Midget Village," a walk-through attraction that took up the entire tenth floor of the store. In what may be regarded as an intentional parody of mass merchandising's artistic pretensions, the all-midget cast featured an elocutionist, a pianist, actors and actresses, and a Santa Claus.[19]

By this time the envelopment of shopping with artistic display was well underway in the airy atriums of Chicago's Marshall Field & Company and the Philadelphia store erected by John Wanamaker. Wanamaker's mercantile interests had taken off years earlier with the lease of a one-time railroad terminal adjacent to the Centennial Exhibition of 1876 that he rechristened "Wanamaker's Grand Depot." While it would appear at first sight that Wanamaker's emphasis upon efficiency might give short shrift to decoration, Wanamaker preferred to think of the exposition-style display of his stores' sales floors not as decoration, but as art. Much as Wanamaker's hero Alexander T. Stewart had done in New York in the 1860s, Wanamaker built his block-long Philadelphia store around an atrium that sacrificed sales space for light and air circulation. Designed by Chicago's D. H. Burnham & Company, the architectural firm that had designed Marshall Field's State Street building (including two light wells, one topped with a Tiffany dome), the

Santa's Own Story Book, Kresge Department Store, Newark, New Jersey, ca. 1926. A children's souvenir of a visit to Santa Claus, this department store premium pictured a cornucopia-like surfeit of toys behind a ceremonial arch.

OPPOSITE Wanamaker's Grand Court, Philadelphia, 1927. The display of Gothic tracery, heraldic banners, the madonna and child with angels, and an illuminated star elevated the center aisle into the realm of a religious experience.

Wanamaker store reveled in classicism. Like Field's, its exterior featured granite columns, which gave a sense of permanence. Inside, the latest technological wonders—telegraphs, telephones, pneumatic tubes, and elevators—speeded transactions on the balconied sales floors. Eschewing mere decoration, the founder lavished tapestries, paintings, sculptures, wooden carvings, plaster entablatures, daily organ concerts, and public lectures upon shoppers. "The applied science of retailing," a company history explained, included the "possibility of a great retailing house supplying amusement, inspiration, convenience and some degree of culture to the community."[20]

Wanamaker's ideas about art were most apparent at Christmas and Easter. The choice of materials expressing the founder's vision could be read in wood, stone, plaster of Paris—traditional modeling materials of artistic quality. Materials valued for their theatrical flexibility such as papier-mâché displaced traditional materials only if they simulated their appearance. At Christmastime Wanamaker's messianic media suggested the permanence of a cathedral in which sales counters receded in the comforting folds of Gothic tracery, heraldry, and the Virgin.

In the competitive holiday display environment of New York, Wanamaker's son Rodman Wanamaker relaxed standards somewhat in allowing papier-mâché figures and garlands in the center court of their store. Erected by Alexander T. Stewart in the 1870s, the celebrated "Cast Iron Palace" had been left behind in the northward migration of retail development centered on Fifth Avenue and Broadway in midtown Manhattan.[21] Though John Wanamaker protested that his 1896 purchase of Stewart's legacy had been based upon a sound consideration of pedestrian traffic, at heart it was not. Wanamaker's purchase may be best understood as a matter of sentiment for the activities and operations of a retailing legend. It would not be the last time that someone mourned the passing of a major department store, including Wanamaker's own.[22]

More than others in New York, the Wanamakers had sound reason to make a holiday spectacle of their store that they enlarged to two city blocks in 1906. At Christmastime, display manager W. F. Larkin set the scene in the store's toy department. For several years Larkin had led the exhibition and display department of John H. Patterson's National Cash Register Company, specializing in visual aids for eye-minded selling. In an era in which department stores placed greater emphasis upon mechanized toylands than cash registers, Larkin staged increasingly complex holiday shows at Wanamaker's from around 1912 into the early 1920s. In 1920, for example, Larkin's *Santa's Circus* became the first animated circus presented to the public in lieu of live performers and animal acts. The walk-through attraction featured mechanical clowns, monkeys, balancing acts using poles, another using a table and a ladder, a bareback rider, an elephant band, a trapeze act, a strong man, jugglers, a lion tamer, performing seals, and a mechanical Santa Claus seated in a private box. The *Merchant's Record* reported that the

"wonderful aggregation of events all going at once… set thousands of children all agog."[23]

Macy's accomplished its move from Fourteenth Street to its present location at Herald Square (Broadway and Thirty-fourth Street) in 1902. Perhaps because of the reduced scale of the new store's windows, Macy's ended its relationship with the Eden Musée, whose specialists had manufactured the animations for the store's "mechanical panoply tableaux." The store continued, however, to mount scaled-down though no less extravagantly staged "revolving windows."[24]

Not until 1923 (perhaps feeling the competitive snap from downtown rival Wanamaker's) did Macy's revive the mechanical panoply tableau, elaborately staged and popularly received as a destination in its own right. That year the store hired Tony Sarg, the celebrated children's illustrator and champion of the marionette theater, to create an animated window feature. Sarg quickly became the agent of an annual holiday build-up that gave Macy's a popularity from which its competitors never recovered. Stripping away the interior walls from a series of five windows mid-block on Thirty-fourth Street, store display men created an expansive setting of some seventy feet for an uninterrupted mechanical panoply display conceived by Sarg. The tableau-type setting presented twenty-six animated fairytale scenes featuring Ali Baba and the Forty Thieves, Alice in Wonderland, Cinderella, Little Red Riding Hood, and Humpty Dumpty. In no time the public spilled off the sidewalk before the windows. The *Merchant's*

Record's F. F. Purdy noted that despite its mid-block location, many "would go out of their way to view the show." "Nothing of this kind has been seen since the days of the famous Macy Christmas windows down at the old location at Fourteenth Street and Sixth Avenue," wrote Purdy. "This revival of the old idea of big toy carnival windows at Macy's has proven a big success." Moreover, "It hooks up in the minds of multitudes with the old Macy windows, which were the delight of New York thirty years and more ago. . . Everybody who sees it tells somebody else, and the throngs, far from the shopping center, grow and grow, on the endless chain plan."[25]

The department store was the place where many Americans received their earliest and most impressionable exposure to novel displays, sublime exhibits, and special effects that became knitted into the city's social fabric. While the miracle and wonder of animated display had been discovered as a motivator, in the end, memory became the most powerful motivator of all, as much a part of that social fabric as the actual experience itself. Every thirty years or so a new generation recalled what had been and what it meant.

Writing a memoir of his experience as chief executive officer of Wanamaker's New York, Grover Whalen recalled working his way through law school as a part-time sales clerk, and later returning to run the enterprise as the right-hand man of store president Rodman Wanamaker. Whalen's memoir was not about store policies, merchandise, or its far-off downtown location; rather, it was about the art and entertainment that made the store more than a store—in fact, an institution. Rising to the occasion, Whalen balanced the life of a store executive with his duties as New York City's official "greeter" for Mayor Jimmy Walker. In this capacity Whalen did as much as anyone to integrate the store into the festive life of New York, overseeing the construction of a triumphal arch for servicemen returning home from World War I, an exhibition celebrating the New York Tercentenary of 1925, and the tickertape parade celebrating Charles Lindbergh's solo transatlantic flight in 1927. Whalen tried hard to impress upon Rodman Wanamaker the importance of relocating the store to midtown Manhattan. After taking in Whalen's closely argued proposal that they move the store to the vicinity of Grand Central Station, Wanamaker informed him that they would not be joining their competitors in midtown. Whalen might have wondered what role sentimental attachments played in Wanamaker's decision. An emotional connection to place could be beneficial in keeping habitual customers, but Whalen believed that Wanamaker's would eventually lose out to their

department store rivals who had followed their customers uptown. For just such a lack of foresight and planning, Wanamaker's New York closed in 1954. The fabled store of Stewart and Wanamaker, Whalen sighed, was "alas…no more."[26]

By the 1920s decorative appearance played an organizing role in defining the store and the amenities of the walking around town, never more so than at holiday time when hearts thawed and sentiment ruled. It was a heady time for the new and novel, for the Christmas store that looked and played the part. Noting the "Boom Christmas Business" throughout the country, the *Merchants Record* reported, "Today the public demand decorations that are in keeping with the holiday spirit and will do their shopping and purchasing in the store that lives up to their expectations in this respect."[27] As the embellishment of the city center proceeded apace, others decorated using newly available electrical materials and invented equally memorable ways to celebrate their creative and special interests with compelling emotional effects.

CHAPTER 3 : NIGHTTIME AT NELA PARK

FROM THE 1920S TO THE 1960S the concerted efforts of display men and women completed the holiday appearance of city centers across the United States. The earliest techniques of flitter and floral tissue evolved into complex decorating schemes that capitalized upon the possibilities of electrical lighting and mechanical animation. The idea that disparate display elements might be combined for an overarching effect inspired specialists who came to champion the free show. Closely associated with the animated window, the free show became a winning institutional strategy among leading retailers who clawed their way back to profitability in the lingering Depression of the late 1930s, when displays made of little more than wood, wire, and papier-mâché contributed to an atmosphere of magical well-being in the walking around town. Ideas about building holiday spirit were widely disseminated through the trade and popular press, and by example in cities and towns that enjoyed long histories of hosting parades and civic celebrations. The adaptation of new electrical products brought movement and flow to the show, experienced through traffic-stopping window displays, spectacular parade floats, and unifying lines of light.

The invention of the electric light and the beginning of a rudimentary electrical service by Thomas Edison in the early 1880s ushered in a new era of possibilities for holiday decor that united light, glass, and color.[1] An expensive plaything, even for those for whom electrical service was available, the lamping of a tree became the much-discussed focus of "electrical Christmas" parties.[2] In the 1910s and 1920s outdoor tree lightings became the rage of municipal Christmas celebrations in New York, Chicago, Denver, and Washington, D.C., where president Calvin Coolidge threw the electrical switch on the first Christmas tree lighting on the Ellipse in 1923. The sixty-foot Vermont fir tree decorated with three thousand lights was a gift from the president's home state. The following year a thirty-five-foot fir tree was planted near the White House in Sheridan Square, with the idea of using a living tree for a recurring holiday feature.[3] General Electric's *Light* magazine noted the popularity of planting evergreen trees for the specific purpose of electrifying them, "a hybrid that bears heavily of an exquisite 'fruit' its very first year," "a magic orchard of colored light."[4]

The seasonal compulsion to decorate with light was never more acutely felt than at Nela Park, the corporate headquarters of the General Electric Company Incandescent Lamp Division in Cleveland, Ohio. Known as the "University of Light," Nela Park mounted its first annual outdoor electrical Christmas display in 1925. Through the years its employees assembled new lighting products and found materials in an unrivaled display that attracted on average three hundred thousand visitors a year. In the beginning the display's ostensible purpose was to demonstrate the possibilities of outdoor holiday lighting effects for electrical utilities, municipalities, and homeowners in general. Yet from the start the display's expansive scope reflected a certain over-the-top and off-the-books enthusiasm for decoration far beyond that of a justifiable business expense. For the workers and managers who imagined and built it, the display held a deeper meaning.

Perhaps such a holiday spectacle could have been anticipated, given the collaborative spirit of education, enterprise, and art that marked Nela Park and its culture. While Nela Park's holiday displays were prototypical, that they occurred on one of the first corporate campuses in the United States made them all the more exceptional. The campus was the brainchild of F. S. Terry and B. G. Tremaine, two electrical industry executives who managed the National Electric Lamp Association (NELA), a holding company of lamp manufacturers. In 1913 Terry and Tremaine relocated their operations from downtown Cleveland to a ninety-acre tract set on a small plateau above Lake Erie, where they built a campus of three- and four-story Georgian-style buildings "thus creating an atmosphere somewhat parallel to that which exists in an institution of the fine arts."[5]

By 1925 with its physical plant complete (including sidewalks heated by underground steam pipes), Nela Park became an outdoor laboratory of electrical Christmas display. The idea of using the grounds for demonstrations of holiday lighting effects came from Orville H. Haas and

Willard C. Brown, two lamping application engineers who were already well acquainted with General Electric's institutional embrace of light as a symbol of progress and social service. The previous summer, for example, Haas had co-engineered an outdoor lighting system for *The Spirit of America*, a pageant staged Fourth of July night in Cleveland's Wade Park.[6] Brown pioneered the engineering standards for outdoor electrical signs and enjoyed a reputation for remedying the lighting problems of theaters. These lines of endeavor converged in prototypical Christmas decor.[7]

With an appropriation of one thousand dollars from the NELA advertising department for a "Yuletide greeting illumination design," the first display appeared Christmas week in 1925. A large "Yuletide Greetings" sign installed across the top of the engineering building beckoned to visitors down the hill and beyond the campus gate. Conveying the motion and fluidity that Brown sought for his commercial work, the sign dimmed to a soft orange glow, then up to nearly red at the top of the arc. "When viewed from a considerable distance," Brown recalled, "the letters appeared to shrink in size as the brightness was reduced and then swell or 'puff out' toward the observer. The attractiveness of *motion* was combined with the effectiveness of *beauty* and a high degree of *individuality*."[8] Augmented with searchlights and stars, by the display's third season it had won an audience of "motorists parked before the gates to watch the great 'Yuletide Greetings' sign alternately swell and dim, to watch the stars sparkle, to let

Entrance gate, Nela Park, 1927. Deploying every electrical device known to modern application engineering, General Electric specialists turned their campus into a laboratory of outdoor lighting effects.

their eyes follow the searchlight beams into space." Never having to leave their automobiles, visitors proceeded onto the campus, "to let the young folks marvel and exclaim at the lighted Christmas trees that studded the grounds."[9]

In the spirit of the outdoor electrical decorating advice given to homeowners urging "individuality," workers devised proposals as managers plumbed the display's limitations as a medium.[10] By 1928 managers had settled upon a formula featuring a "spectacular feature" in front of the engineering building visible from the campus entrance gate, and smaller effects such as

Illuminated ice pile embedded with flashing colored lamps, 1930

a Nativity or trees grouped along a circuitous route through the campus. The opportunities afforded by this plan met the needs of aspiring campus decorators as well as the commercial interests of their contributing departments. Sales department managers, for example, sought to incorporate new lamping products into the display. A new method of light control using "thermionic" vacuum tubes, for example, might regulate the intensity of lamps; similarly, the optical soundtrack of a Photophone might provide the sound of sleigh bells, or cue

sequences of sound and illumination. The same specialist, however, rejected "picture-in-a-frame projections" and similar visual elements that invited comparison with "the fast-moving presentations of the screen."[11]

Specialists described the production with the rigor of a scientific experiment. For example, a review of decorating ideas used in 1930 described the making of an "illuminated ice pile" inspired by an idea entered in an employee design contest. The review noted that the translucent pile "was perhaps the most talked-about feature of the entire display. To most of our visitors, it was the most novel and attractive item." The reviewer methodically noted the percentage of chosen lamp colors, their operating voltages, the rubber washers and melted paraffin that sealed sockets from moisture, lamp failure rates, the problem of settling ice (another ton was added) and the fortunate fact that low temperatures kept the pile frozen through New Year's. Despite the installation's popularity with the public, specialists chose not to repeat it.[12]

The careful evaluation of the features of each annual display weighed aesthetic choices and their supposed impact. While specialists did not shy from traditional religious themes and symbols, they typically characterized as "modern" the overall impression that they wished to convey. These included the snow-covered cottage built of illuminated flats, and the stylized Christmas tree mounted to the facade of the engineering building, which became the central features of the display in 1927, accompanied by twin searchlights positioned on the roof above. Specialists also used the term "modern" to indicate a lack of "festoons," that is, unadorned light strings draped between poles or placed on trees. Many of the same specialists looked down upon the outlining of buildings with strings of socket sets, preferring a nighttime fantasy that bore little resemblance to architectural reality.

By the early 1930s the making of the display became more like the planning of a drive-through experience. The study of holiday visitors led one specialist to propose "an arbor or series of

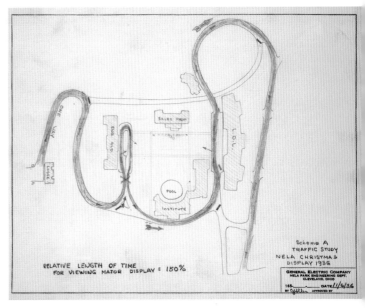

Traffic study map, 1936. Specialists paced the motorist's progress through the display believed to be the first drive-through attraction of its kind.

archways...[that] would satisfy the craving of people to be part of the parade." Another noted that even the most "spectacular feature" could be scaled down for home use.[13] In many cases the display's effect transcended its underlying commercial purpose. One Cleveland resident set down this sentiment in verse. Martha J. Francis, a nurse living on Terrace Road a few doors down from the campus entrance gate, composed an homage entitled "Behold, the Star!" The first and last stanzas of her eight-stanza appreciation spoke to the display's personal effect. Francis wrote,

From my window to the eastward,
Gleams effulgent beauty, rare;
Seems a hand Divine had built it,

OPPOSITE TOP Campus entrance and Lodge, 1936. Located just inside main gate, specialists decorated the interior of the campus Lodge to appeal to homeowners.

OPPOSITE BOTTOM Brochure, *Suggestions—Ideas—Materials*, 1937. Photographs of campus displays illustrated an inexhaustible supply of how-to literature directed to the attention of store and shop owners.

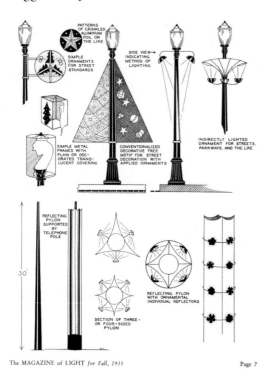

Suggestions for STREET DECORATIONS

The MAGAZINE of LIGHT *for Fall, 1935* Page 7

"Suggestions for Street Decorations," reprinted from *Light Magazine*, Fall 1935

Cast it forth into the air.
Colors shifting, shadows playing,
All in rhythmic motion are;
While the crowning burst of glory,
Looms above — "Behold, the Star!"[14]

While many visitors may have regarded the display as magical, if not divinely inspired, its creators noted that the real magic lay in the volume of visitor traffic traveling the campus night after night.

Specialists wasted little time in claiming the display's popularity as a creative advantage. Holiday time offered "unlimited opportunities" for "expressive imagination," needing little more than the ingenuity of arrangement and color made possible by the relatively low cost of electrical decor. Urging that Christmas displays be made rather than bought, campus lighting engineers never tired of noting new and inexpensive construction materials that could be used to this end—composition board, metal foils and sheets, plastic sheets, translucent fabrics, natural and artificial floral materials, colored lamps, and floodlights. The idea of literally "creating the holiday spirit" became a key component of General Electric's Depression-era promotional campaign entitled "Prosperity Avenue" that envisioned a "new business street" where "trade follows light."[15] Photographs of Nela Park's holiday displays filled trade literature that took up the promotional burden in the early 1930s. Increasingly this literature pictured holiday spectacles from outside the confines of the campus, featuring construction

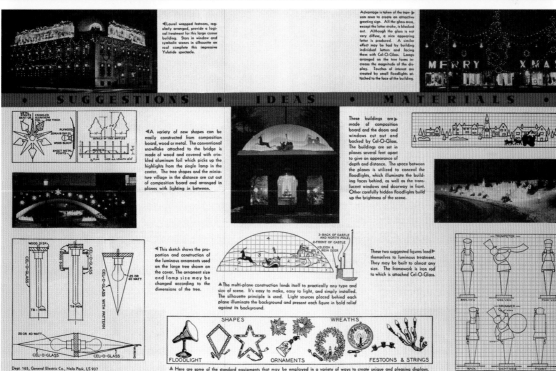

OPPOSITE Engineering building and illuminated trees, 1949. Using artificial firs, cut evergreens, and an occasional live tree, specialists created a greeting card-perfect drive-through spectacle.

plans for street lighting and store interior displays, and noteworthy examples of illuminated store facades and outdoor displays sponsored by electrical utilities and municipalities.[16]

During the Second World War, Nela Park went dark and did not resume its annual Christmas show until 1949. The show's seven-year absence was attributed to material shortages. The display's return reinvigorated the tradition of the all-campus spectacle made by employees who capitalized upon every material advantage known to application engineering. That year specialists built a sixty-foot artificial tree around a utility pole, a design very much like that used in the display's last outing in December 1941. The tree carried concentric wood-framed sections covered with chicken wire finished with green plastic boughs, each a wonder of product placement. Offsets concealed horizontal green Lumiline fluorescent tubes projecting upwards on the boughs of the tree. Vertical white fluorescent tubes served as figurative candles.[17]

With the display's return specialists sought to extend its influence by staging a broadcast-ready "special preview lighting" held for an audience of employees and their families. The thirty-minute program was telecast as a local news event on station WEWS.[18] The staging of the event lent new prominence to the display's "spectacular feature," in this case the lighting of the tree. The following year specialists recovered the tree with reflective aluminum to use in the same way. Elsewhere on the grounds, specialists sought to interject more child appeal with "luminous wire men," playfully

Christmas tree construction, 1949. Using new lighting products and familiar construction techniques, campus engineers erected a tree illuminated by fluorescent tubes that encircled a sixty-foot utility pole.

articulated wire figures standing in for the real-life engineers who "worked over ornaments and last minute decorations that were being carried up the hill to the big tree by more of Santa's helpers."[19]

By 1952 specialists had framed the display as a drive-through "Christmas album" that dispensed with the spectacular feature. Instead of a single focal point, specialists staged four "greeting card" scenes picturing domestic life and fashions set in 1878, 1903, 1928, and a two-part 1952 setting picturing *Santa Today* and the *Christmas Home of Tomorrow*. The "home of tomorrow" appeared to be remarkably like the home of today, with allowances for popular tastes that favored (in spite of illumination engineers' disdain) building outlines and festooning. Among the ideas shown were "ways of outlining one's house effectively by night," "festooning windows and doorways," "trailing strings of gem-like lights over shrubbery," "adorning the tree at the living room picture window," and the final touch, "crowning one's 'peace on earth' with a home-spun snowflake star." As a press release helpfully explained, "Here, the Yuletide spirit, expressed through lights, is carried out in a manner which anyone may apply."[20] Anecdotal comments seemed to confirm that visitors warmed to "the novel effect and the simplicity with which they could produce similar results in their own homes."[21]

Having overcome their aversion to subjects that invited comparison to the cinema, in 1953 specialists framed a twenty-two-by-twenty-four-foot "greeting card" "living room scene." The shadowbox setting featured yuletide symbols of the "traditional fireplace with filled stockings," the "glowing tree," and backlit silhouettes of "entranced children gazing wide-eyed from the staircase hoping to catch a glimpse of Santa." Figures of elfin workmen in stocking hats adjusted the frame of this and other displays. The opening night program featured congratulatory remarks by company officials and a live musical performance by Bing Crosby, who formally lighted the display via a specially leased wire from Hollywood and sang the perennially popular "White Christmas" by Irving Berlin, the centerpiece of the feature film, then in production with Crosby in the starring role.[22]

Such overpowering showmanship threatened to turn the display into a show about a display, but it remained the domain of the lighting application engineer. As late as 1958 there was still room for modernist display elements, each a prototype with a parts list and a plan for making it. Specialists took great delight in mounting novel and attractive display elements whose premise need be nothing more than "a number of lighting techniques." Well into the late 1950s the campus favorite was the luminous shadowbox "greeting card" with clever spill light effects.[23]

What effect did the display have beyond the specialists who created it, or campus visitors from greater Cleveland, northern Ohio, and surrounding states who flocked to it year after year? Drawing upon a 1956 market analysis report, company officials believed that their efforts on behalf of outdoor Christmas lighting over the years had now begun to "catch hold" with the public. For years the number of homes using outdoor lighting had remained stable at fourteen percent. In 1955 that figure jumped to twenty-two percent, an increase that specialists attributed to the popularity of home decorating contests, rather than the decoration of Nela Park.[24] Company officials began to wonder if the display's annual budget of fifty thousand dollars could be justified. In part the answer was yes, but it could no longer be driven by anything other than the inspiration of campus engineers, given the proliferation of comparable commercial and residential holiday displays outside its gates. Instead of citing Nela Park's display as the last word in holiday lighting, company marketing specialists now took pains to explain that creating a custom designed lighting scheme was no longer a factor in mounting a successful display. The elements could now be purchased and installed by a commercial decorating service, an electrical utility, or a sign company. Relieved of having to explain the intricacies of building display elements from scratch, specialists turned their attention to explaining the importance of community fundraising to purchase or rent decorations installed by a contractor, whose fee could be prorated "among the sponsoring merchants on a per foot basis."[25]

During the holiday season of 1958, company officials began to formally reconsider the effect of their display. In many ways the display had become a victim of its own spectacular success. Its popularity had devoured the neighborhood at the campus's Terrace Road entrance, now choking on traffic that queued up to snake

Shadowbox greeting cards, 1958

through the illuminated grounds night after night. Local residents no longer composed poems of appreciation. They threatened lawsuits. With the growing acceptance of holiday lighting from those very residential side streets to shopping center parking lots, the display could no longer be justified as a marketing tool. In 1959 officials reluctantly closed the campus to drive-through traffic, moving a token display to the campus fence line along Noble Road—enough of a display to be seen by passing motorists, but not enough to stop and linger over.

The closing of the campus to holiday traffic and the relocation of the display to Noble Road was a matter of animated discussion within the company. As A. L. Barr explained, "it seems to me that the big job of establishing Christmas lighting in business areas has been well accomplished and consequently there is less need for massive displays on our part. And certainly…the traffic situation has been getting worse."[26] While Barr and staff thankfully noted that there had been little adverse public reaction to the decision to close the campus and relocate the display, they did seek to mitigate the impact of their decision by announcing that henceforth Nela Park's decorating efforts would be decentralized to GE's Cleveland area industrial plants.[27] After a few years, however, the program quietly closed down. It had never been easy to support from the campus, and the results, for lack of far-flung engineering talent, were mixed. Public reaction to the downsized display mounted along the Noble Road fence line was not. Disappointed passersby wondered if GE had gone out of business. Recognizing their mistake, the following year officials emptied a warehouse of past years' display elements onto the property, installing every electrical device and light-up prop that could be pressed into service along the five-block fence line.

The Noble Road display continued on its own terms, more so for the new generation of lamping engineers and designers who carried on the company tradition of technological accomplishment with a personal touch. Frank LaGiusa, a recent hire from New York's Lightolier Corporation, found himself designing the display in 1966. "I had been

to Nela Park before," recalls LaGiusa, "but never at Christmas." Unaware of "the legend," LaGiusa was led to a file of photographs dating to the earliest installations of the 1920s and given the job. He set to work visualizing a theme: "Lollipop Park." Shortly after the display's installation along the campus fence line, LaGiusa and his young daughter lingered among the giant illuminated treats. "They looked so real to her," he recalled. "She asked, 'Daddy, can we pick one?' For me, that was vindication of the work."[28] After that LaGiusa never failed to consider the role of the audience in "scenes to be viewed, scenes to be occupied" and the mobility of the audience, "making them viewers of one scene, participants in another, or both simultaneously." Whether rendered by an amateur or a professional, the marvel of it all was that "the will to display… somehow gets expressed."[29]

From its inception in the 1920s, Nela Park's annual holiday display had acknowledged the will to display as a personal rather than a business function. Even on a reduced scale the display's historical significance could not be denied, whether in inspired nighttime displays across the nation or across the front yard, beckoning in ways both large and small.

CHAPTER 4 : MECHANIZATION TAKES COMMAND

AS THE POSSIBILITIES OF ELECTRICAL DECORATION became established in the early 1920s, the use of small electrical motors to animate papier-mâché figures had only begun to develop as a creative medium of holiday display. In the massive toy departments of downtown retailers, animated displays became an acceptable substitute for live circus acts. The spectacle of the circus, however, never caught on with retailers who pursued more subtle effects to burnish their stores' prestigious identities. Their attitudes about display animation began to change in the mid 1930s, enlivening what Lord & Taylor's Dorothy Shaver described as the "free show."[1]

From the 1920s through the 1960s the animated display evolved from a circuslike attraction into an expressive medium for institutional selling and storytelling. The firms of Messmore & Damon, and Bliss Display Company, the two most influential companies of the period, made animation a winning business, each in its own way. Messmore & Damon bridged the lurid pleasures of the sideshow and the carnivalesque interests of business pageantry. Bliss Display, responding to the creative goals of department and specialty store clients, elevated the Christmas window to an institutional art form.

"AMPHIBIOUS DINOSAUR BRONTOSAURUS"
41' IN LENGTH — 9½' IN HEIGHT — MOVES MECHANICALLY. REQUIRES TEN
MOTORS TO WORK EYES, HEAD, NECK, HIPS, STOMACH, SIDES AND TAIL.
THE ORIGINAL SKELETON IS AT THE AMERICAN MUSEUM OF NATURAL
HISTORY — NEW YORK CITY.   MESSMORE & DAMON-INC.
                                          404-8 W. 27th ST. N.Y.CITY.

LEFT Joseph Damon
(left) and George Harold
Messmore with their
largest animated
creations, 1930

BOTTOM Historical
Parade float staging area,
Hudson-Fulton pageant,
Central Park West and
110th Street, New York,
1909

The partnership of George Harold Messmore and sculptor Joseph Damon reversed the usual course of commercial development from window to float. The Messmore & Damon Company ushered in a renaissance of papier-mâché manufacturing in New York City during the 1920s, beginning with float construction and moving into the manufacture of window display props. Messmore hailed from Detroit, where he began his career as a theatrical scenic painter and a prop and gadget maker. Joseph Damon, a butcher's boy from Mt. Vernon, Illinois, attended art school in St. Louis. After four years of study Damon won a scholarship to the prestigious Art Students League on New York's West Fifty-seventh Street. Both Damon and Messmore rode the rails to New York to seek their fortune.[2]

The future partners became acquainted while working as float builders for New York's Hudson-Fulton pageant of 1909. Schooled in papier-mâché modeling techniques by the New Orleans float designers especially imported for the occasion, Messmore and Damon found gainful employment among the one hundred sixty artists, modelers, decorators, and mechanics who turned out one hundred four parade floats for the pageant's Historical and Carnival parades, the most elaborate ever staged in New York.[3]

The pair formed a "hit-or-miss partnership" traveling the country "building any kind of decoration that anybody wanted, anything from a triumphal arch to a plaster elk."[4] After five years of itinerant display jobs (during which they split up for a time while Messmore went to work for Detroit's

MESSMORE & DAMON, Inc.
404–408 West 27th Street, New York

No. 20. MODERN VASE
4' in height

No. 9. GREEK VASE
3' 6" in height

MESSMORE & DAMON DESIGNS COPYRIGHTED

Papier-mâché vases for window and interior displays, Messmore & Damon, ca. 1921

Cadillaqua pageant and struggled with contracts for San Francisco's Panama Pacific International Exposition) they resettled in New York. Winning float construction contracts for World War I bond drives and the celebration of the Armistice in the late 1910s, they determined to build a predictable demand for display work with a line of artistic papier-mâché vases and urns that passed for the decorative onyx, marble, and plaster artworks favored by department store display managers. But vases and urns were soon overshadowed by the line that Messmore later described as the basis of their fortune: animal figures animated with electrical motors.[5]

Messmore's emphatic note is instructive, for it underscores the serendipitous nature of display at the moment that it became a sustainable

Messmore & Damon exhibit, Annual Convention of the International Association of Displaymen, Chicago, 1922

occupation. Damon, the partnership's lead artist and "inside man," sculpted the figures. Messmore, the tinker, artist and "outside man," added motors and sold them. They created figures on spec—with only a general idea about who might purchase such a thing, or how it would be used. Messmore sold their first animated papier-mâché figure to a department store—a monkey that stuck out its tongue. A competitor took note and ordered the firm's second figure, a donkey that wiggled its ears and kicked its legs. Needing little in the way of further encouragement, the partners gleefully proceeded up the food chain from monkeys and donkeys to cows and elephants, pausing only after making a robot pachyderm that could curl and uncurl its trunk, heave its sides, ruffle its ears, and bat its eyelashes.[6]

Though hardly the first to create an animated figure, Messmore & Damon excelled in marketing their lifelike creations. They made five elephants for impresario Florenz Ziegfeld that humbled one theatrical reporter who erroneously noted the Follies' use of live animal acts. A figure's promotional value rose in proportion to the playful context in which it appeared, often unexpectedly and frequently unreal. For the 1931 New York auto show, for example, the partners mounted an elephant figure atop a Chrysler to demonstrate the strength and solidity of the car's body. The elephant-car operated in the streets outside the show at the Grand Central Palace. The performance resulted in telephone calls and letters from the New York Humane Society objecting to the inhumane treatment of the beast. "Really," wrote one observer,

Messmore & Damon's animated elephant mounted atop a Chrysler, New York Auto Show, 1931

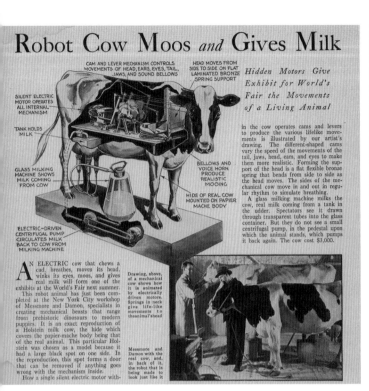

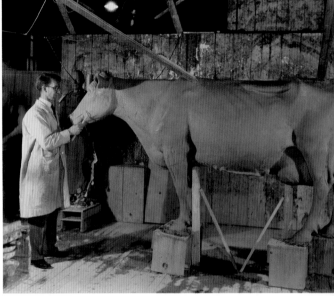

TOP LEFT Messmore & Damon's "Robot Cow" became the stuff of popular science at the Chicago Century of Progress, 1933.

TOP RIGHT Joseph Damon models a clay figure, the first step in the papier-mâché process.

BOTTOM RIGHT The completed cow and milking machine, 1933

"it looks what it purports to be and the deception is enhanced by the wagging of the elephant's ears and trunk, made possible by a small motor concealed in the interior." The same elephant followed the auto show to Philadelphia, Detroit, and Chicago.[7]

The emotional value of a figure sometimes became apparent before it left the shop. In 1932 representatives of the McCormick-Deering company (manufacturers of farm equipment) contracted for a mechanical cow with which to demonstrate an automatic milking machine at the Century of Progress, the world's fair opening in Chicago in 1933. Agreeing to take the job, Messmore & Damon facilitated its client's search for an ultimate specimen to model. A Holstein was located and purchased from a New Jersey dairy, and brought to Messmore & Damon's Chelsea workshop on Twenty-seventh Street. A concrete stall was especially built and outfitted for the animal, which arrived with its own attendant courtesy of McCormick Deering. The attendant milked the cow daily, with the milk going to neighborhood children who, never having seen a cow, showed up on the doorstep to take in the scene with cups in hand.

Damon set to work sculpting a full-scale clay likeness of the cow from which plaster casts for papier-mâché positives were taken. The casts were then filled with papier-mâché that when dry were sewn together and sanded smooth. Damon, the former butcher's boy, had the cow slaughtered and skinned, stretching its hide over the completed papier-mâché form. When word got out that the "dark deed" had been done, workers invited the children to see and hear the finished model mooing, breathing, contentedly chewing her cud, and swishing her tail. The workers bought fresh milk to ladle out until the figure left the shop for its new exhibit home at the Century of Progress.[8]

The emotional impact of the partners' mechanical figures played from audiences of neighborhood children to department store display executives, theatrical property managers, and trade reporters who regarded the shop as the most unusual manufacturing plant in the country. In any given year one might encounter the construction of floats for Macy's and Eaton's of Canada's Thanksgiving Day parades, floats and exhibits for the Baltimore & Ohio Railroad's Fair of the Iron Horse, holiday treatments for store facades, and the animated circus figures that displaced live acts in department store toy towns from New York to Chicago in the early 1920s.

More than a curiosity, Messmore & Damon, became a magical place of business. As one reporter noted, "These workers, most of whom are highly paid specialists, seem to think it is fun to turn out such diverse products as a fairy castle and a gorilla—and no doubt it is. One leaves the factory regretfully. It is a place in which to relive one's childhood. It is a whimsical, individual place—a standing refutation of the statement that only the standardized can succeed today."[9] The shop, enthused another, "Would be the delight of both the museum director and the child."[10]

Though Messmore & Damon never realized a market for animated figures in a museum,

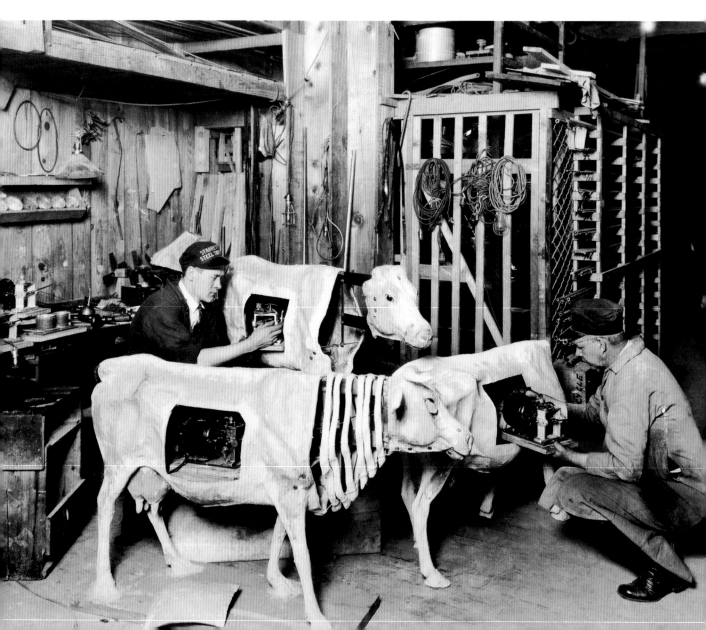

OPPOSITE, CLOCKWISE FROM TOP LEFT Messmore & Damon workers applying plaster to clay models, for plaster molds that will be lined with papier-mâché; workers lining plaster molds with papier-mâché. A single plaster mold could be used indefinitely, producing multiple papier-mâché casts. Plaster molds are stored for future use, above; mechanics installing electric motors in papier-mâché figures, ca. 1935

BELOW Diagram showing the operation of Messmore & Damon's *The World A Million Years Ago*, Chicago Century of Progress, 1933

am Showing Operation of Exhibit Depicting World a Million Years Ago; Spectators Will Be Carried through the Dome-Shaped Structure on a Moving Concourse or Sidewalk

Dioramas with Mechanical Figures in Action Show the Various Ages of Man, and in a Pit Are Grouped Huge Prehistoric Beasts and Reptiles Actuated by Motors; Note Control Room

the life-sized mechanical dinosaurs that they pioneered between 1925 and 1933 won praise from paleontologists Roy Chapman Andrews and Walter Granger of the American Museum of Natural History. In late 1931 Andrews and Granger toured the partners' shop, praising the beasts that later appeared in *The World A Million Years Ago*, an attraction that the partners operated at the Century of Progress. The gestation of the show's idea began on a New York City sidewalk where the partners visualized the framework of a "huge prehistoric monster" in a steam shovel excavating a building site.[11]

The visualization of a dinosaur came at an opportune moment for Messmore, whose determination to animate the largest living creatures to ever roam the earth was as much a matter of pride as the logical extension of a product line. Messmore explained, "The monkey started my fortune. The donkey came next, and when we built an elephant the [Detroit] merchants who bought them as advertising novelties said I'd reached my limit. But I decided differently."[12] The partners first modeled a *Brontosaurus* (scientists now call it *Apotosaurus*) based upon a fossil skeleton collected by Granger that had been exhibited in the American Museum of Natural History since 1906. One-third the size of the actual specimen, the twelve-foot-long figure first appeared in the lobby of New York's Astor Theater where it promoted a feature film based upon Sir Arthur Conan Doyle's *The Lost World*. The model later created a riot when it was booked into a Newark department store toyland where it attracted four hundred thousand visitors.[13]

Explaining their figures' appeal, Damon noted that two distinct kinds of movement were required to attract and hold the viewer's attention. First, a figure needed a sweeping motion (such as the neck movement of a dinosaur) that caused the viewer to stop. After that, the viewer lingered over small operating details such as a raised eyebrow, a dilating eye, or a twitching tail. Messmore suggested that the psychological source of the public's fascination with their animated figures could be found in the human appetite for transcendent experiences like those at Coney Island.[14] In fact, the beasts played Coney Island's Surf Avenue amusement zone alongside Messmore & Damon attractions recreating the hokum of Barnum's *American Museum* and the partners' macabre *History of Torture*, which for understandable reasons was not booked in department stores during the off season.[15]

The emotional effect of Messmore & Damon's work contributed to the burgeoning medium of display animation and its professionalization in the late 1930s. In his 1937 *Yearbook of Motion Displays* editor I. L. Cochrane noted that the "animators" of Baum's day had been succeeded by "animation engineers." "Contraptions of wood and wire, like the one-cylinder car, have long since passed into the limbo of pioneer efforts," Cochrane wrote. Cochrane cited the application of "engineered architecture with stamina and lasting beauty" in exhibit venues ranging from world's fairs to local window displays.[16] Prominent animated display manufacturers included the Old King Cole Papier Mache Company, of East Canton, Ohio, and the Gardner Display

Poster, P. T. Barnum's American Museum, Messmore & Damon, 1940. The partners idolized Barnum, and recreated his famous humbugs (featuring a talking figure of Barnum himself) as a fitting tribute to his showmanship. Their packaged attraction debuted in the Amusement Zone of the New York World's Fair in 1940, and later toured department stores.

Company, of Pittsburgh, Pennsylvania. The Old King Cole Company was the merger of three papier-mâché companies dating to 1887.[17] In the late 1930s the firm became a Disney licensee. Its holiday display sets included a "Snow White" wishing well into which children spoke and magically received a complimentary gift from Santa.

The Pittsburgh-based Gardner Display Company began in a one-room sign shop in 1918. Company founder and former steel company chemist William Marshall Gardner branched out

from painted to electrical and neon signs. Impressed by the trend in exhibitry that he saw at the Century of Progress, Gardner quit sign work for the field of display animation. Gardner Display specialized in the creation of mechanical talking robots used in fair stage shows, including a twelve-foot-tall talking *Alice in Dairyland* for the Wisconsin Centennial and a twenty-three-foot-tall talking Paul Bunyan for the Chicago Railroad Fair. The firm created animated window features such as the "Weather Makers," an interpretation of natural phenomena acted out

A sequential animated display depicting weather: Rain Makers (**OPPOSITE**), Wind Makers, Lightning Makers, Snow Makers, and Rainbow makers, Gardner Displays, ca. 1938

Christmas Display Dramas, Bliss Display, 1940

by elves operating machines with the behind-the-scenes cachet of a workshop cutaway.[18]

While Messmore and Damon, Old King Cole, and Gardner Display drew inspiration from the tradition of the barker, the sideshow, and the business pageant, displayman James Albert Bliss found inspiration in artistic animation effects that joined store and street. Bliss leveraged the raucous carnival temper of animated display into the emotionally charged environment of "visual merchandising," an expression that he coined in 1941. Demonstrating little use for the circus or the operational aesthetic of the factory cutaway, Bliss's window work furthered the fantasy qualities of display. His creations took up traditional storytelling that unfolded like a story on a sidewalk.

An artist and amateur historian, Bliss published prolifically in *Display World*. In a 1944 review of Thomas D. Clark's country store monograph *Pill, Petticoats and Plows*, for example, Bliss repeated Clark's observation that "the store at Christmas time was literally a meeting place of stark everyday reality with a fantastic world of temporary but pleasant escape."[19] The juxtaposition of reality with fantasy distilled the meaning of Bliss's holiday displays that bracketed the Second World War. Bliss's work confirmed the institutional value of display animation among department and specialty stores, and it was here that he built his reputation.

Born in Abingdon, Massachusetts, in 1902, Bliss appeared on stage at the age of eight with his vaudevillian parents. Like George Harold Messmore, Bliss found stagecraft more compelling than acting. From Evander Childs High School in New York City he won a scholarship to the New York School of Fine Arts (now Parsons), studied drafting at Columbia University, and painting at the Art Students League with John Sloan.[20] In some ways Bliss never left the theater in which he grew up. He often explained that his window sets for Lord & Taylor, Macy's, and others were simply larger versions of the theatrical models that he had once made.[21]

Bliss received his most lasting lesson in business showmanship from Lord & Taylor vice president (and later president) Dorothy Shaver. In the 1930s Shaver had first conceived of dramatizing fashion themes in the store's show windows, and Bliss had won the job of creating them for store display manager Dana O'Clare.[22] Shaver had long complained about the monotony of "window trimming." She was the first, Bliss recalled, "to strive to get out of the rut. She started with merchandise. She complained about its placement. Her instructions were to get away form so-called 'balanced' trimming. 'Throw it from the ceiling if you must, but get away from formula. I want an element of surprise about our windows.'" In response O'Clare launched an angular style of attack. Lord & Taylor's competitors joined in and the new style soon became a rut itself. "Lord & Taylor had started all of this, yet, its promotions had slipped into a formula. Miss Shaver became restless. The pressure was started. Christmas was approaching."[23]

The resulting *Bell Windows* established a new pattern of institutional merchandising without merchandise, a deceptively simple idea that fulfilled Shaver's leading desire for a "free show." Created by O'Clare, developed by Bliss, the show featured large papier-mâché bells covered with golden tinfoil gently swinging above a snowy landscape dotted with artificial fir trees in the store's Fifth Avenue windows. The bells tolled to the distant sound of muted chimes. Sashlike ropes connected to hidden electric motors provided the movement, while speakers connected to a concealed amplifier and turntable delivered the sound to the sidewalk.

By all accounts Lord & Taylor's bell windows awakened and instilled a new appreciation of

Bell window display by Bliss Display for Lord & Taylor, 1937–1941. The symbolic ringing of bells over a snowy landscape dotted with trees became a cultural phenomenon and institutional touchstone, the quintessential "free show" of department store holiday display before the Second World War.

display among store executives and an appreciative public. Originally scheduled to run for just five days, the display ran for a month up to Christmas day. The store reported some four hundred thousand comments confirming the popularity of show windows utterly devoid of merchandise. *Display World* could not resist noting that the whole affair had cost two thousand dollars, a paltry sum when compared to the outpouring of favorable comment, the foot traffic pulled into the store, and increased sales over the previous year's holiday season.[24] Bliss wrote that the show's popularity "made miserable

The Christmas Book

John Wanamaker

PHILADELPHIA

THE GRAND COURT, PHILADELPHIA
Symbol of the spirit of a great institution.
The meeting place of all Philadelphia.

the life of every displayman in New York City. And the rest of the country. 'Do something like Lord & Taylor—or something better.' Display received its place as a really important part of the store's promotional life."[25]

The display's impact upon Bliss's fortune was just as immediate. The following November Bliss outfitted Lord & Taylor with "snowstorm" windows for a winter coat promotion. Again, the windows presented no merchandise. The windows achieved their effect with a frosting of beer and Epsom salts solution. A circular portion of the glass was left clear at the center of each window. Through the opening could be seen a "snowstorm," actually bleached corn flakes blown about by a concealed hair dryer. Display cards read, "It's coming—sooner or later." A blizzard howled over the sound system previously used for the bell window display. Unveiled on an unseasonably warm November day, the windows caused a run on the store's stock of winter wear. By week's end a real snowstorm had moved into New York City, and a wondering press chalked it up to the prophecy of Lord & Taylor. *Snowstorms* by Bliss played simultaneously in store windows in fifty-eight cities. Bell window installations followed in sixty-three cities, including Lord & Taylor New York, the first repeat of a display theme in recent memory. The bell theme played equally well in the Grand Court of Wanamaker's Philadelphia. With a stopover in Paris at Galeries Lafayette for an Easter show in 1939, the bell windows struck a note of optimism in a war-weary world from 1937 to 1941.[26]

While the bell windows had hit the mark, Bliss's "snowstorm," however, elicited a protest from retailing's Fifth Avenue Association of which Lord & Taylor was a member. The association's leadership feared the cheapening of the avenue's high-toned atmosphere with animated features better suited for the midway than the windows of specialty stores. While Lord & Taylor president Walter Hoving agreed in principle with the association's ban on motion displays, Hoving stated that "we cannot permit anyone to tell us what we can or can not do with our windows."[27]

Display World invited Bliss to tell about the method of the country's most successful display business. Bliss had become a phenomenon by establishing a "high market for display with high-priced personnel." Bliss's studio staff included department heads represented by a stage designer, an interior architect, and an advertising layout man, each a sketch artist capable of producing "thoroughly workable ideas and sketches for an advertising display." The department heads reported to a "coordination manager" aided by an assistant responsible for reporting merchandising trends and who combed all markets for "existing merchandising conditions and future trends."[28]

Paul Gianfagna, the son of Bliss art director John Gianfagna, recalled Bliss's Thirty-fourth Street workshop as "quite a space." The elder Gianfagna had taught his ten-year-old son how to get from their home on Staten Island to Hell's Kitchen by subway to spend the day at the shop. "I was terribly intrigued by the environment," Gianfagna recalled.

OPPOSITE Bliss's animated window features sometimes appeared to break through the glass itself, if only metaphorically, bringing the viewer into the store. In this example, children drop their letters to Santa into a dead-drop box mounted on a window, while directly on the other side of the window a moving conveyor belt appears to move letters from the box, through the glass, past an animated Santa figure wielding a postal cancellation stamp. Bliss's clever animated feature appeared at Macy's in 1948 and throughout the country in 1950 and 1951.

"It was truly magical for me. It impressed me no end. The three-dimensional figures—they moved." As a young man Paul Gianfagna went to work for Bliss as a scenic artist and later joined the graduate faculty of the Brooklyn College Art Department. Recalling his introduction to the creative process as a youngster, Gianfagna enthused at the revelation that "one could imagine something, make a drawing and build it." The treat was watching "the people who related to it." The experience "drew me into the area of art that sustains me even now."[29]

One of the most memorable animated features that his father designed was a special mailbox for letters to Santa. Actually a dead letter drop mounted on an outside window, the device left the impression with casual viewers that a conveyor belt carried letters through the window into the store. The illusion spoke volumes about the removal of barriers between the store and the street, in this case embellished with a mechanical Santa, wielding a cancellation stamp.[30]

Bliss was driven to imbue display with this purposeful message. As display men grappled with their professional identity on the eve of America's entry into the Second World War, Bliss came to believe that the word *display* was lacking as an occupational descriptor. "Display" failed to convey the varied tasks of "visual selling" such as "fashion shows, civic visual presentations, and War Bond drives." Bliss was inclined to the expansive interpretation of responsibilities that went beyond so-called "ribbon tying" to bottom-line functions such as sales and store planning. Much

as "trimming" had been displaced by "display" in the 1910s, the rhetorical shortcomings of "display" had become apparent. In its place Bliss offered "visual merchandising," a phrase came to mind when Bliss received a letter from the U. S. Office of War Information's "Division of Visual Information" requesting a bid for propaganda displays.[31]

Bliss characterized the animated features of the home front holiday window as "visual merchandising." By 1944 Bliss's research divined that "patriotic red white and blue" Christmas themes had run their course. Thereafter, Bliss's holiday window sets favored "homespun and early American Yule" themes featuring holly, bells, Santa Claus, and red and green color schemes. Neatly folding the underlying logic of the theme into the new sales responsibilities of visual merchandising, Bliss described "The Origins of Christmas Customs" as "the most attention absorbing Christmas Promotion ever produced!"[32]

After the war, as Chairman of the National Association of Display Industries Display Research Committee, Bliss wrested a small budget to study the habits of window shoppers. The resulting survey of window display traffic made by Professor Howard Cowee of New York University's School of Retailing asserted display's value as an advertising medium, and led to a curriculum in visual merchandising techniques. With the evangelical fervor of an efficiency expert, Bliss explained that display and store planning were one and the same—responsible for "everything store traffic sees or should see."[33]

By 1950 Bliss had produced Macy's Christmas show for ten consecutive years and had rolled out

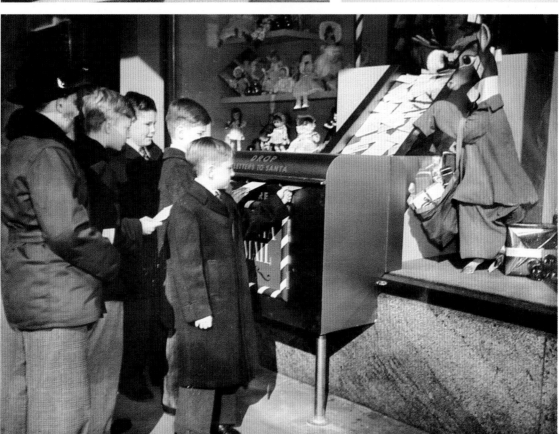

multiple copies across the country to hundreds of clients. Bliss promoted that year's feature, entitled "To Grandfather's House for Christmas," as a "soul satisfying, homey Christmas show." "See all the animals in Grandfather's barn having a gala Christmas…see the bossy Stable Dog…the old Goat dressing up as Santa…a volume sales producer of toys and store-wide gift merchandise designed to fit all budgets."[34] J. P. McEvoy, the novelist, playwright, and roving editor of *Reader's Digest*, cited Bliss for retail stagecraft that emptied wallets: "They make you buy things you don't want with money you haven't got to give to people you don't like." *Display World* reiterated, "In a nutshell this is what Bliss has been trying to do for 25 years…sell more people more goods faster, through an emotional appeal to own goods on impulse."[35]

Traditional Christmas themes and settings once driven by the uncertainties of war offered balm and solace as Bliss advanced the cause of "visual merchandising" after the war. By insisting that display be acknowledged as a source of sales, Bliss noted, the displayman would gain a larger portion of the store's advertising pie. To the extent that display became a function of postwar store planning, its future would be assured. That it remained the "poor sister" of rival advertising media in the store's budget was puzzling. Perhaps, Bliss suggested, display suffered a lack of respect and a corresponding budget because it was the one advertising medium that the store itself owned and operated. The logic of this observation appealed to Bliss, who had done as much as anyone to provide an intellectual basis for display study, modeling, and testing. However, Bliss did not anticipate the way in which that very information served the business model of the open-shelf, self-service retailers who demonstrated little interest in display as Bliss defined it.

By 1950 it appears to have dawned on Bliss that he had undercut his case for visual merchandising by emphasizing the cold reality of empirical data. Revisiting the gestation of the idea in 1951, Bliss noted visual merchandising's progress in the measurement of effects and the development of a curriculum by Professor Cowee at NYU. But, Bliss wondered, "in acquiring a new language, are we now in danger of losing our native lyrical tongue, which is and always will be the language of inspired, imaginative showmanship? It is a language of creative make-believe that our customers had always understood…even if foreign to statistic-minded planners." Bliss never again visited the history of his idea in print; instead, he zeroed in on the shortcomings of "planners" who appropriated "visual merchandising" in name only, distorting its meaning beyond recognition in stripped-down retail outlets that "let the merchandise speak for itself." One could sense the amenities of "business art" slipping away, "imprisoned in an unvarnished, literal and heartless super-market of merchandise exposed on efficient trestles, embellished only with show cards and price tickets."[36]

Though "planners" removed barriers between consumers and goods, Bliss noted, "they will not sell more goods to more people unless they recall a prime psychological fact…namely, the desire to own almost anything starts with an emotional appeal." This had always been the function of the holiday display in the walking around town, and it is interesting to note how Bliss's displays—as much as they may seem to be about traditional, familiar themes—can be read as a comment on the disconnect of merchants who divorced themselves from the responsibilities of display as Bliss understood them. Bliss's 1956 holiday offering, for example, promoted the idea of "your town." Expressly addressed to the downtown retailer, It's Christmas in Our Town built upon the popularity of "old fashioned heart-warming Christmas T.V. programs last year…proving that the American public WANTS an old-fashioned Christmas. OUR BIG CHRISTMAS ATTRACTION this year…It's Christmas in Our Town will capture the hearts of everyone in YOUR TOWN."[37]

As Bliss continued his case for "downtown survival" into the early 1960s, one could hear the plaintive echo of Dorothy Shaver ordering up a free show. Seeking to stanch the influence of the suburban shopping center that had "captured the imagination and dollars of its community, at the expense of the downtown trading area," Bliss urged his clients to organize holiday display efforts around a common theme: "Christmas Is a Family Affair Downtown."[38] And for a time, Bliss's animated holiday displays enjoyed continuing success where animated window sets conferred a certain pride of leadership among retailers. Bliss retained Lord & Taylor as a client into the 1970s, and performed

notable work for Macy's Herald Square, constructing an elaborate holiday facade for that store in 1959. The two-and-one-half-story-tall feature fronted the Broadway section of Macy's building with backlit shadow-box animated figures and settings in European cities. Supporting columns from the sidewalk showcased Nativity scenes.[39]

Though the subtle charms of animated holiday display soldiered on, the free show fell noticeably short of expectations as retailers reevaluated their merchandising strategies. The shopping mall, with its relentless focus upon unencumbered displays of merchandise, became the new model for the packaging of Christmas display elements with the full-time amenities of art, water features, landscaping, and parking. The central administration of seasonal amenities in the way of holiday décor enforced a retail identity for the mall rather than individual mall tenants.[40]

Seeking to enlarge its shrinking client base with new business removed from retailing, for a brief moment the Bliss Display Company joined Messmore & Damon in the amusement business as the major contractor of rides and exhibit elements for Freedomland, U.S.A., a Bronx theme park conceived as the East Coast's answer to Disneyland. Freedomland folded up in a matter of years, due to poor planning and competition from the 1964 New York World's Fair.[41]

The complexities of television production became the mainstay of Messmore & Damon. At the time of his death in 1961, George Harold Messmore was working on mechanical game

Rendering and plan elevations by John Gianfagna, Bliss Display, for Lord & Taylor, ca. 1960–1970

CLOCKWISE FROM TOP LEFT *The Candy Tree; Happy Eskimo; Backstage Christmas Party; Christmas is Giving*

LEFT Finished window display by John Gianfagna, Bliss Display, for Lord & Taylor, 1964

BOTTOM *A Fantasy of Christmas*, Bliss Display for R. H. Macy & Co., 1959

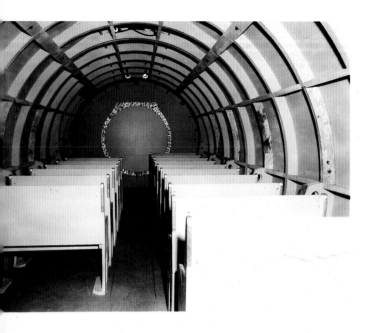

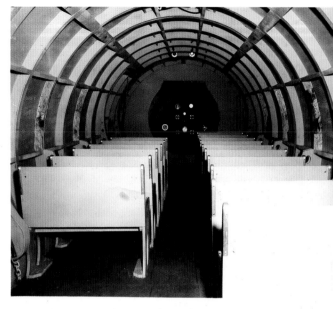

MESSMORE 2

pieces for the NBC television game shows *Tic Tac Dough* and *Concentration*. However, his heart as well as his firm's was in display. Francis G. Messmore, his son, took over the business, making annual tours of Lake George, New York; Connecticut's Danbury Fair; and other outlets looking after the firm's colossal figures and attractions. Francis Messmore said goodbye to the large dinosaur figures of *The World A Million Years Ago*, unpacking them from storage in a New Jersey warehouse, selling some to a Chicago wax museum entrepreneur who later sold them to an amusement park in Japan. The firm continued to dabble in stand-alone amusements booked into department stores at holiday time. In December of 1951, for example, the firm built a large spaceship for interplanetary travel exhibited at Gimbels Philadelphia store. The ship took thirty passengers on a trip to Mars in eighty seconds. Gimbels' Christmas draw proved so popular that store officials posted the premises with signs: "Adults must be accompanied by children."

Whereas display firms such as Messmore & Damon taught the carnivalesque merchandiser to play, James Albert Bliss animated the free show and taught it to pay. In time, visual merchandising became closely associated with the self-service concepts practiced by discount retailers whose stores showered consumers with a surfeit of goods, but demonstrated little of the theatricality that Bliss had championed. A transitional figure in the history of display, Bliss occupied the high ground among retailers who understood display as an amenity, and the retailers who questioned its relevance in the postwar era. Increasingly the high ground was circumscribed by the success of discounters who disavowed display as an unnecessary business expense, and whose stores showed it. By 1959 the expression "sad heart at the supermarket" had been put into play as a visual shorthand for the mediocrity of American consumer culture.[42] As stores struggled in downtown locations and suburban rivals cut costs, the saddest heart of all belonged to James Albert Bliss.

CHAPTER 5 : FLOATING SPHERES OF INFLUENCE

IN THE FIRST DECADES OF THE TWENTIETH CENTURY the commercial methods of parade float construction became available throughout the United States. Circles of style radiated from cities where builders had developed regional, seasonal businesses including New Orleans, Pasadena, New York City, Miami, and others.[1]

By this time "floral architects" had become experienced at decorating vehicles of all kinds.[2] Lauding the artistry of America's civic pageantry, critics cited tableau-type floats for their smart use of materials and their colorful, harmonious effects. Horse-drawn buckboards, trailers, and hay wagons, for example, became mobile stages saluting workers and their occupations. The workers who mined the coal—or caned the chairs, or reaped the harvest—created the float upon which they and their product appeared, often decorated with little more than a swag of bunting and a herald-type banner. Cut flowers and agricultural by-products such as cornstalks became symbols of abundance and fecundity that doubled as decoration.

Between 1900 and 1940 float designs gradually shifted from producer-oriented displays, that showcased work and industry, to consumer-oriented fantasies that typically showcased home

TOP LEFT Chair caners, Medfield, Massachusetts, ca. 1900. Created by those who rode with them, turn of the century floats often presented facsimile production processes and products.

TOP RIGHT United Mine Workers of America anthracite coal float, Dubois, Pennsylvania, Labor Day 1908

LEFT *Ceres* float with corn husk coverings and Ohio state banner "Farms for Sale" (left); carriage with floral tissue covering (right), ca. 1925

RIGHT S. B. Call toy store floats, Springfield, Massachusetts, ca. 1909–1910. The masking of floats with floral tissue diminished the role of merchandise with symbols, such as this sleigh, that sold the idea of the store.

and community life. Floats shed work as a subject, just as they masked vehicle wheels and operating features. The last vestige of labor seen in the line of march was the horse and driver required to move the float down the street. Two photographs picturing the floats of S. B. Call, a Springfield, Massachusetts, toy merchant, suggest how this symbolic makeover was accomplished with floral sheeting. The photographs are believed to have been taken in successive summers in Springfield around 1909. The first shows Call on his delivery wagon piled with toy carriages and sporting goods, topped by a Teddy bear on a rocking horse. The second pictures Call in a Santa suit on the same wagon transformed into a sleigh. The occasion (perhaps the Fourth of July) for which Call's floats were made cannot now be determined. The photographs suggest that even modest floats such as Call's abandoned the catch-all clutter of nineteenth-century merchandising for more focused and arguably more memorable display concepts in the first decades of the twentieth century.

The modern float papered over mechanical operating features with carnivalesque tissues, trims, and cut flowers. An alternative to flowers and garlands, floral sheeting held certain advantages as a masking material. It covered seams to give the float a unified appearance. It could be mass-produced and sold in rolls. The introduction of the automobile into the line of march was readily accomplished with floral sheeting. The Chicago Artificial Flower Company,

Tournament of Roses. New Year's Day. Pasadena, California. BOARD OF TRADE FLOAT

Postcard, Isabella Coleman's Pasadena Board of Trade float, Tournament of Roses, 1913. The comprehensive masking of vehicles with cut flowers was noted by parade spectators, as was the inadequacy of pictures that conveyed the effect. The writer of this postcard explained, "This gives you no idea of how lovely the float was, but you can see how solid the work is—you could see nothing of the auto save a bit of the wheels near the ground. The flowers were lovely, not dull colors like this card."

for example, circulated catalogs of float designs and covering materials that explained how to decorate a Model T.[3] The colorful effect was a paper-thin rebuttal of the dictum attributed to Henry Ford: "Any color so long as it's black." The idea was to forget the machine underneath the airy froth of floral tissue.

Indulging the fantasy required keeping one's feet on the ground while nearly everyone else took holiday. Leroy F. Vaughn, who marketed float kits for do-it-yourselfers in the 1950s, favored the float description of a veteran parade chairman for whom the ideal was "a tethered cloud, curved and billowing, looking substantial yet floating light as

air." Isabella Sturdevant Coleman, the leading float builder of Pasadena's Tournament of Roses, devised steel undercarriages to lower the "cloud" to the knee level of curbside spectators. Bill Tracy, Macy's resident float builder, strove for the "light fantasy touch" using sculptural plastics. Noting the sales resistance of cost-conscious parade sponsors and publicity directors, Tracy mused that the sale of any float began with an "elaborate, dreamy sketch, leaving much to the imagination."[4]

One of the foremost float builders in any generation, Isabella Coleman was typical in the serendipitous way that she happened into business. Between 1913 and 1965 Coleman created over three hundred floats for the Tournament of Roses. Her reputation grew with the parade and its sponsors who competed for her prize-winning floral fantasies. Pasadena's sun-drenched pageantry valued individual expression and civic participation, and in this climate one might just as easily have become a builder as a spectator. In the interviews that she gave throughout her storied career she recalled decorating her first float with her mother in 1904 at the age of twelve.[5] Pasadena's New Year's Day parade was completely woven into the fabric of the region's middle-class life. To decorate and ride was to belong. Known to her friends as "Izzy," Coleman first rode on a school float in 1908. In 1910, however, she could not find a place. Heartbroken, she explained her predicament to her parents, who suggested that she enter a float of her own. To her lasting surprise her own *hoss and shay* decorated with marigolds and greenery won second place in the "horse-drawn

conveyance" category. Thereafter she was never without a float—or three or four—on New Year's Day. As a courtesy to her father, she built floats for the Pasadena Realty Board, winning a tournament cup for best "motorized carriage" in 1913.

Her winning reputation did not go unnoticed. On the recommendation of tournament officials, the Los Angeles Chamber of Commerce summoned her to discuss a float for the 1914 parade. Upon meeting the twenty-one-year-old Coleman, chamber secretary Frank Wiggins was taken aback. "Why you're just a little girl," he exclaimed. "We wanted a man." Coleman replied, "I can build your float and decorate it too." Her enthusiasm for over-the-top decoration was rewarded with the tournament's top award, the Anniversary Challenge Cup.[6]

Though Coleman considered herself to be a part-time businesswoman, her business model made no distinction between her personal life and her ambitions as a community-minded float builder. The entire operation ran "out of her head," recalled son David Coleman. "When she would get a contract she would put money into her personal account for the contract. When the year was over, the bills were paid, if she had money left over she made a profit. If she made no money, and lost money, then she had a loss." The financial significance of her dealings hit home during the Depression when her husband, David Sr., a banker, lost his job. David Coleman recalled "when my father lost his job…she first became aware she'd been making any money— because she'd just been sinking it into the family joint account, and paid no attention to it. When

TOP Rendering, Queen's float by Isabella Coleman, Tournament of Roses, 1934

LEFT Preliminary rendering, for Coleman's City of Los Angeles float, 1935

Isabella Coleman with steel structure for *World Peace*, the San Diego City and County float for the 1965 Tournament of Roses, the last parade for which she built floats.

that happened she suddenly realized that she was supporting the family because he wasn't supporting it. I mean, her financial dealings were amazing."[7]

Coleman is widely acknowledged for establishing the all-floral extravagance of the Tournament of Roses. The floral covering evolved over time from the parade's early days, when builders wove or tied flowers to their vehicles, often using smilax, a commercially grown vine used for window displays. Smilax could be shaped into garlands or applied as a base covering into which fresh cut flowers could be inserted. Coleman was the first to paste flower blossoms on a float in 1929. The ideal float was floral, self-propelled, and low to the ground. She excelled in the design of steel undercarriages welded to truck frames outfitted with large-capacity radiators, hidden cockpits for drivers, and small-diameter airplane wheels that enabled the finished float to hover just above the street. The fantasy that made blossoms come alive for spectators was her triumph.[8]

Work started in late March or early April after tournament officials announced the parade theme. Coleman typically drew from fifty to one hundred designs, often sketching several versions of an idea for the same float. She drew inspiration from a wide range of sources, from paintings to magazines to clouds in the sky. She described her ability to zero in on design elements as "keyhole vision." For example, a dragon borrowed from a magazine advertisement for a pain reliever became a favorite float motif; a cloud formation inspired a swan, and so on. She took her sketches to a commercial artist in Los Angeles who painted renderings showing what the finished floats would look like. Never knowing what might come in handy, she never threw drawings away. She amassed so many that she was forced to develop a literal in-house filing system, "under my rugs," where "they lay flat and stay fresh." Similar ideals informed her presentation of her floats to Tournament judges before the parade on New Year's Day. "I try to make my floats look as finished as if they were going on my dining room table," she explained. "The judging isn't done from the sidelines—much of it is close inspection."[9]

By early summer 100 to 150 concepts would be winnowed down to just 10 for the 6 or 7 sponsors with whom she negotiated contracts. Construction commenced in October in a city-owned Quonset hut on Lincoln Avenue just east of the Rose Bowl. The hut was one of two buildings built by the tournament for float construction, given to the city, and leased back to the tournament that then rented space to float builders. Coleman persisted in viewing the enterprise as a community project begun with paid part-time labor and completed with volunteer armies of "petal-pushers" who worked into the wee hours of the morning on New Year's Day. Construction began with Coleman chalking the outline of the float's footprint on a one-by-one-foot grid permanently marked on the floor of the hut. Engineer Jimmy Iwanaga interpreted Coleman's designs, which she conveyed in chalk outlines, drawings, renderings, and verbal instructions. Iwanaga produced drawings for the steel rebar superstructure that took the skeletal shape of a

I Love a Western float by Walter Garbett, 1956. Garbett's creation featured galloping horses bursting from a large television set to the delight of its young viewers, as Roy Rogers and Dale Evans appear knee deep in the pages of a book.

pagoda, a dragon, or other form. The rebar was then "cocooned" with window screening and spray-on polyvinyl foam. When dry the foam was painted and keyed to the appropriate floral covering applied not more than forty-eight hours before parade time. The process was never finished. David Coleman recalled, "As floats were being built she would develop ideas about which ones were likely to win prizes, to be more beautiful. She would dip into the bank account, go out, and buy more orchids." These might be added, for example, as lei-style blossoms strung from the rebar roof of a pagoda or placed in liquid-filled test tubes inserted into the cocooning.[10]

    From time to time Isabella Coleman wondered aloud that she might retire. When she contemplated retirement, however, she thought again. "The difficulty," she admitted, "is that I keep getting new ideas."[11] She left the parade at the height of its powers in 1965. In later years she preferred watching it on television. She left a competitive design environment fueled by some eighteen builders and the interests of their commercial sponsors. There was plenty of work, limited only by tournament officials' determination to keep the parade to two hours using no more than sixty floats. A waiting list of sponsors wanted in on a good thing—a national telecast with a receptive audience of seventy-six million viewers. One sponsor divided the cost of his float by the total viewing audience to come up with the "world's greatest advertising bargain" at .0000523 cent per person.[12] Coleman poured their advertising dollars right back into her floats, increasingly using animated display features

Frozen Fairyland float by Matt Offen, Valley Decorating, 1951. Offen's float featured an ice rink, the first of its kind. Although Tournament of Roses floats must be completely covered with flowers, Offen received special permission from officials for the use of ice. The tree branches were decorated with 75,000 sweet peas; the trunks with 75,000 Vanda orchids, 1,000 full-sized orchids, and 3,000 red and yellow roses. The float bed was covered with white chrysanthemums and hundreds of delphiniums, mums, cornflowers, camellias, lilies of the valley, and roses. Skating champions Helen Legge, Mickey Bel Isle, and Barbara Jones performed throughout the parade.

calculated to attract the lingering attention of the television cameras.[13]

Builders joined in the fun of topping one another. Longtime builder Walter Garbett, for example, created *I Love a Western*, a float with an enormous television receiver from which leaped a rollicking stagecoach and team. Roy Rogers and Dale Evans stood waist-high in the flattened pages of a giant book mounted in the foreground. Matt Offen, a new builder from Fresno, devised a low-slung ice rink that rolled down Colorado Street with performing Olympic skaters. The refrigeration engineering was as impressive as their performance. When Offen asked his wife, a native of Pasadena, what she thought of his triumph, she replied with a question of her own. "Why can't you make floats like Isabella Coleman's?"[14]

The tradition of the floral float cherished in the memories of Pasadenans withstood the pressures of commercialization, for the tradition's maintenance depended upon volunteers who appreciated the finished effect in more ways than television could convey. Giving a tour of floats in the latter stages of construction in 1951, Coleman paused to consider the volunteer workers from the city of Gardena, half a dozen adults and a dozen teenagers bending wires together. "That float was designed by the citizens and schoolchildren in Gardena, and it is being built by them, too," Coleman noted. "It's all free work and so they can put that much more money into flowers. It's going to be one of the best floats in the parade. But what is more important than that is the fact that those people

are building a lot of personal pride and satisfaction into the float. Regardless of whether it wins a prize, there's going to be a lot of people from Gardena strung along Colorado Street on New Year's Day who will say, 'That's my float!' when it goes by."[15]

Coleman's ideas about voluntarism—without which even a commercially produced parade could not succeed—explains how parade participants and spectators reconciled its pleasures with that of the home television viewer who might be forgiven for thinking of the parade as the world's longest commercial. It was an odd tension, but somehow it worked. Experienced in person, the spectacle packed an emotional wallop. The telecast multiplied the parade audience many times over for the sponsors who increasingly paid the bills.

The possibilities of making a creative living in display were never more wide open than in the postwar era of the commercial parade, and there was no better example than the Macy's Thanksgiving Day parade. In 1953 Macy's contracted for float design and construction with William T. Tracy. Between 1951 and 1954 Tracy created novel props for Ringling Brothers in Sarasota, Florida, and his fans at Macy's regarded him as the ideal man for their job. Capitalizing upon new plastics and resin coatings, Tracy's work bridged the parade and amusement park fields, before his business came to ruin in a haze of alcohol and unpaid taxes. He was by all accounts an outgoing and flamboyant personality, described as brilliant in his field. Amusement park operator Randall Trimper, who purchased a Haunted House ride and a Pirate's Cove

Tracy's sculptural floats
and props as seen in *The*
Greatest Show on Earth,
Ben Walters, Inc., 1952

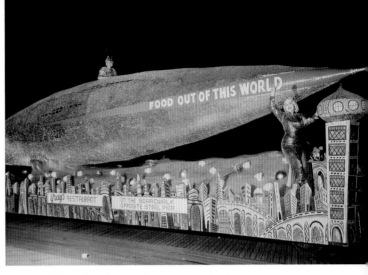

Food out of this World, Miss America Pageant, Atlantic City, date unknown. Tracy designed this float for Macy's, after which it appeared on the Atlantic City boardwalk as an advertisement for a restaurant. As built by Bob Noedel, a track and ball system activated by a spring mechanism elevated and lowered the rocket to and from launch position as it traveled in the line of march.

funhouse attraction in the early 1960s, recalled that "Tracy could just walk in, tack up a few strips of wood, paint it a fluorescent color, and make something happen."[16]

Hailing from Toledo, Ohio, Tracy came to national prominence in the pages of *Display World* magazine, where he described the rough and tumble requirements of the circus props that he had made using a new plastic fabric, "Celastic." An improvement upon papier-mâché, "Celastic" could be molded and sculpted in great detail into any shape. When hard, the piece could be painted. Impermeable to water, the piece could withstand exposure to the elements, without fear of disintegration by rain, snow, heat, or cold.[17]

Declaring Tracy to be "the best man for the job," Macy's E. A. Hill locked up Tracy's services for parade and display work for ten thousand dollars a year for five years beginning in 1955. What cemented the deal was the imaginative finish of Tracy's plastic work, his desire to settle down with an affiliation and, for both Tracy and Macy's, the profit sharing of outside display contracts. A unique feature of the contract allowed Tracy to perform work beyond that which was needed by the store. The net income from such work, which was considerable at the time, was turned over to the store, tallied up at the end of each year, and split fifty-fifty between Tracy and Macy's. Thus Tracy had the incentive to earn more than his ten thousand dollar annual fee, while contributing in a positive way to the store's balance sheet.[18] Outside orders on the books in 1955, for example, included props

for the traveling *Holiday on Ice* show for which Tracy created a set, a volcano, chandeliers, and drums; and the Rye, New York, Playland children's park for which Tracy created a whale, castle, Noah's Ark, a giant, a gingerbread house, and a post office. All told, the jobs netted some forty-four thousand dollars.[19]

The subsequent sale of Macy's floats after their use in parades contributed to the store's and Tracy's bottom line as well. The artistry of Tracy and lead modeler Bob Noedel attracted willing buyers in the eastern United States. Display man Earl Hargrove and his father Earl, Sr., for example, sought out Tracy's and Noedel's work. "Tracy made the most beautiful stuff you ever saw," Hargrove recalled. Most memorable was a rocket ship animated with an internal spring and ball mechanism that raised and lowered the ship to and from launch position. The Martian surface beneath the rocket glowed with

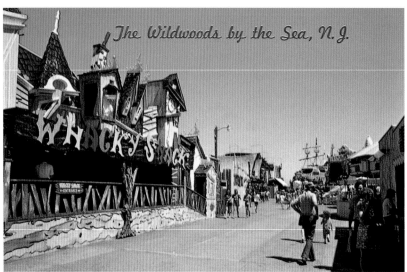

TOP Tracy's ark and rocking horse floats for Macy's at rest in his New Jersey float studio, ca. 1956

LEFT Tracy's *Whacky Shack*, Hunt's Pier, Wildwood, New Jersey, 1964–88. The whimsical framing of Tracy's floats informed the "fronts and stunts" of his dark rides.

back-lit jewels and rocks.[20] A skewed perspective distinguished Tracy's most playful work. An ark with a giraffe poking through a squared off hole in its roof, for example, featured signature off-kilter window and door frames, as if the builder had been on a bender. In later years the riotous framing of architectural details would become familiar to enthusiasts of Tracy's amusement dark rides, that were informed by his experiments with fluorescent black-light floats made for Bamberger's, Macy's sister store in Newark, New Jersey. For Bamberger's first Thanksgiving Eve parade in 1955, Tracy created a luminescent parade set off with ultraviolet projectors. The city turned off streetlights along the mile-long parade route in order to achieve "trick effects" alternating between incandescent and ultraviolet light. Tracy's Cinderella, for example, "changed from rags to riches and her pumpkin and mice turned into a handsome coach with horses."[21]

Nagging questions of liability dogged Tracy's contract work with Macy's from the start, as store executives soon found themselves in the amusement ride business with Tracy. Should anything go wrong, the store could be held liable. A new agreement retained Tracy to build floats and display props for Macy's on an annual fee basis of seventy-five hundred dollars. The rest was up to him.[22]

The take-off of Tracy's now classic darkride and funhouse business dates from the Bamberger parade and the renegotiation of his contract with Macy's. From then on, Tracy was in business as the Tracy Parade and Display Company and soon organized the Outdoor Dimensional Display Company. Both companies used the same Liberty Avenue address in North Bergen, New Jersey. The development of new darkride features was informed by the fluorescent paint and masking techniques that Tracy pioneered for the Bamberger's parade. But instead of black-lit features that rolled past the spectator on the street, the spectator got into a car mounted on a track and rode by them. The characteristically off-kilter features of Tracy's imaginative float work were readily applied to the "fronts and stunts" of the rides, featuring wildly out-of-plumb ticket windows and other frenetic details, while the "stunts" inside typically featured out-of-control buzz-saws, flushing toilets, black-lit bats, and the blinding glare of a suddenly switched on locomotive headlight and horn, all prefaced with a disorienting ascent through a slowly revolving cylinder on a twisted track that gave the impression that one was turning upside down. Sculptor Manfred Bass, one of the first artists that Tracy hired after rearranging his priorities with Macy's, recalled the motto of Tracy's fluorescent workshop: "We work in the dark!"[23]

By the parade season of 1963, Tracy's business had begun to unravel. He had failed to keep up with taxes. With no notice and with precious little time left to produce that year's parade, one September morning Noedel and Bass came to work and found themselves locked out on the street. Overnight, Bass recalled, "the government had slapped a padlock on the door, and we were out of a job." Macy's eased Tracy out of its Bergen workshop and helped him find a warehouse for float storage for which Macy's

OPPOSITE TOP Earl Hargrove's *Adlai-Ike* float, President's Cup Regatta Aqua-Pageant, Washington, D.C., 1952

OPPOSITE BOTTOM Santa arrives in style at the Washington Redskins halftime show on a Hargrove float with a calliope, Washington, D.C., 1959

paid rent. Tracy was instructed to remove his tools and equipment from Bergen and the Macy's Herald Square display department took over the space.[24]

The dispersal of his talented company was Tracy's final act as a Macy's contractor. Macy's Dennis Mulhearn hired men and bought materials needed to complete that year's Santa float and a Jack and the Beanstalk push float.[25] Tracy relocated to Cape May Courthouse, New Jersey, where he returned to the darkride business in the years before his death at the age of fifty eight in 1974. Bob Noedel resettled in Cheverly, Maryland, to spend the rest of his career with the Hargrove Company in the company of several of the floats that he had made for Tracy. Hargrove's Washington, D.C.–based float circuit extended to Philadelphia and Atlantic City; down Maryland's eastern shore; across to Winchester and Richmond, Virginia; south to Atlanta, Georgia, and to Mardi Gras celebrations in Shreveport and New Orleans, Louisiana. Manfred Bass accepted Mulhearn's offer to head Macy's float-building and display operations. Tracy had turned the black light float in on itself in fluorescent darkrides with multiple viewing levels. Bass turned the darkride inside out and back to the float. Bass's "multidimensional viewing perspectives" emphasized sculpture and live talent, turning the float into a theater-in-the-round ideally suited for parade telecasts.[26]

While the Macy's parade made ongoing accommodations for television, the business of creating floats and float designs became an enterprise of national proportions. Though

TOP Parade staging area, Washington Monument Centennial Celebration, Washington, D.C., 1948

BOTTOM Stockings modeled by mill workers, the Story of Salem Pageant, Salem, Virginia, 1952

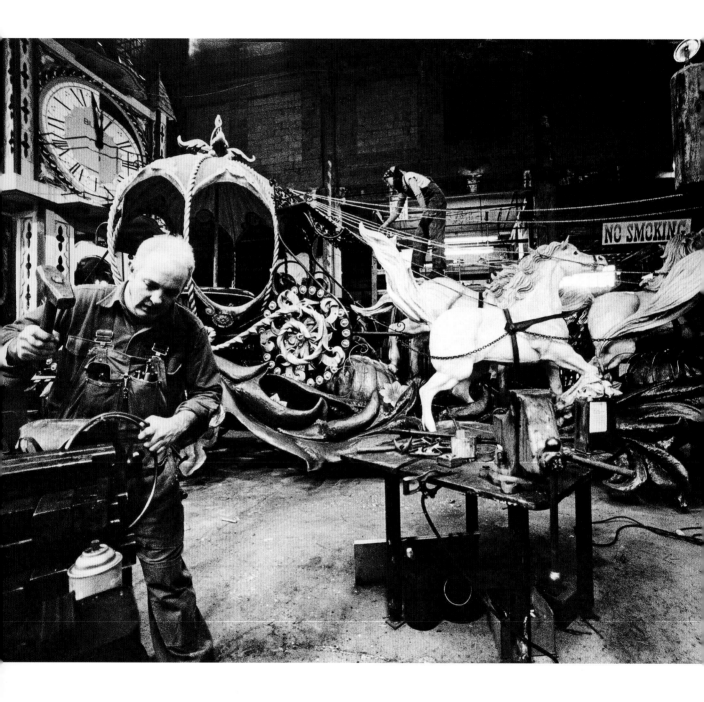

Float builder Manfred Bass in Macy's parade float studio the day before the annual Thanksgiving Day parade, 1980

Hargrove, Inc. float studio exhibition of U. S. Bicentennial Parade floats, Landover, Maryland, 1976

Catalog centerfold, *Celebration Days*, Vaughn Displays, Inc., Minneapolis, 1956

no one can state with certainty the number of float builders working at the time, in 1956 one observer estimated there to be 170 builders whose creations satisfied local and regional appetites for commemoration and celebration.[27] Leroy F. Vaughn, a Minneapolis float builder who graduated to parade management and discovered a lucrative market for float kits, found that "no place, it seems, lacks a reason for celebration. It can be a crop, or a product, or a natural feature, or a historic incident, or a mineral resource. It can be mining, manufacturing, agriculture or culture…the variety of themes now given annual airing is bewildering."[28]

Incorporated in 1949 to manufacture commercial display and parade float supplies, by the mid-1950s Vaughn Displays Company was the world's largest manufacturer of parade float kits. The kits, created by Cyrus A. Krake, Vaughn's chief designer, mechanic, tinkerer, and inventor, became popular with amateur builders as well as display professionals. The kit idea was rooted in Vaughn's experience in display sales and Krake's experience as a young float designer for the Minneapolis Aquatennial, a night parade that began in 1940. The Vaughn parade circuit extended from Minnesota to Florida. A native Iowan, Vaughn began his career as a door-to-door salesman. He opened a window display service in Ft. Lauderdale, Florida, in the mid-1930s, and discovered his calling with the floats that he built for the city's Labor Day parade in 1935. Through his display work Vaughn became acquainted with Ernest E. Seiler, a prominent booster of all things Miami. In 1937

Aerial view of the King Orange Festival Parade, Miami, ca. 1955

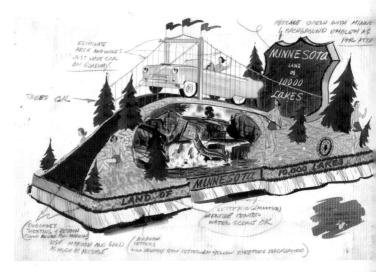

Seiler conceived what became the annual Orange Bowl college football game and linked it with the Palm Festival parade, later entitled the King Orange Festival. Both game and parade were run straight out of the Depression-era playbook of promotional strategies that created public spectacles from sparse resources cobbled together with voluntarism and community pride. Woodrow Wilson Westberry, who joined Vaughn in creating floats for the 1937 Palm Festival, recalled that their method began with a trip to the junkyard. "For $25 you could buy a Cadillac or LaSalle, build a frame around the car, reinforce strong points where the girls could sit, one here, one there, 4-5-6-7 girls." With the city's blessing Vaughn and Westberry built floats under Miami's Twelfth Avenue Bridge. They later moved to a succession of abandoned industrial buildings rented from the city, including a roundhouse in Hialeah and a seaplane terminal on Dinner Key. By 1948 the construction of some forty floats for the King Orange Festival—the city's marquee event held on New Year's Eve—had become a year-round activity.[29]

Until then most floats were made locally. By the early 1950s Vaughn was packing them into boxcars in Minneapolis and shipping them by rail to Florida where they could be trailered from Miami to other cities for reuse with minor modification. This practice reduced costs and made money by multiplying the stock of floats available for use in a given locality. This proved to be a boon in South Florida where the floats made for the King Orange Festival went on to appear in Bradenton, Sarasota, and Tampa. From Tampa

TOP Newspaper cartoon, Orange Bowl parade, 1947

BOTTOM Rendering, *Live and Play in Miami* float, King Orange Festival Parade, ca 1960

many were exported to Havana, Cuba, where they appeared in Carnival parades. Krake recalled that the Cuban officials sent to take delivery of floats in Tampa preferred that they be built over brand new American cars. At dockside the officials stuffed them with consumer goods, "every modern device known to man."[30]

It was Krake's job to come up with an annual innovation in animation. In 1950, for example, Krake devised a mechanical hummingbird that flew forward and in reverse. The following year he improvised a seagull, mounting six of the birds, each with a ten-foot wingspan. "While one gull flapped its wings in flight," a reporter noted, "another glides and soars."[31] A design innovation unique to Miami was the "outrigger," a miniature rolling platform hooked to a float or to its towing vehicle that rein–forced the central theme. A typical scenario featured a float towed by a "boat" accompanied by a phalanx of outrigger water-skiers.

Clever presentation and technical accom–plishment became the hallmark of Seiler's production of the Orange Bowl half-time show, and here Krake served as well. The show's climax came with the unveiling of a mechanical feature whose sole function was the delivery of the festival queen. In 1951 Krake created a telescoping tower using a portable crane extending forty feet into the air. The queen appeared atop the tower, revealed in the fall-away peel of a monumental orange. Historian Arva Parks recalled that Seiler kept the show's theme a secret—"You had to come see it." "You were looking to see where the queen would pop out."[32] The

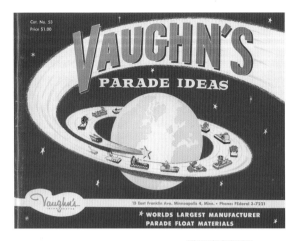

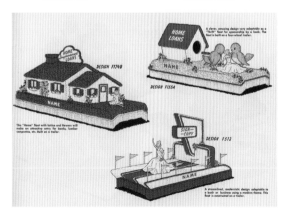

TOP Catalog cover, Vaughn's Parade Ideas, 1958

MIDDLE Automobile decorations, Vaughn's Parade Ideas, 1958

BOTTOM Bank designs, dairy designs, Vaughn's Parade Ideas, 1958

stadium reopened for fireworks and a second show the following evening, where the floats were paraded for the crowd one last time. The floats became so large with outriggers that Seiler tore down a portion of the east and west end-zone stands and fences so that they could be brought into the stadium.[33]

The Vaughn Company applied the do-it-yourself aesthetic of 1950s leisure to the community-oriented tasks of parade float construction. The customer chose a design from a catalog, carefully matching the picture of the desired float with the vehicle upon which it was to be built. By return mail the customer received a blueprint for the construction of an underlying wooden framework, and vinyl floral sheeting in various colors applied as a covering. The only things not supplied were labor, lumber, and the vehicle.

The kit idea recommended itself as a way to stimulate demand for the floral sheeting that Vaughn and Krake manufactured. As Krake conceived it, the "float system" was geared toward the rotating membership of local chambers of commerce whose leaders served an average five-year term. Krake filled the float kit catalog with page after page of colorful designs and insisted that none be retired or taken out, given the expected turnover of chamber officials who became Vaughn customers.[34] Vaughn printed 12,500 catalogs in 1953. In the following year the kit offering became so successful that Vaughn formally quit the float-building business to sell kits.[35]

Under the editorial direction of Krake, the Vaughn catalog turned the parade float into a

LEFT Card file, Vaughn Displays Inc., ca. 1950–1980. Krake's card file was used to fill orders received at company headquarters for parade float kits. An index of popular commemoration and celebration, the file duplicated in a more comprehensive way the designs featured in Vaughn's float catalogs, categorized for any and all occasions.

BOTTOM A modified version of Vaughn Display's float kit #150, Schenectady County Sesquicentennial Parade, Schenectady, New York, 1959

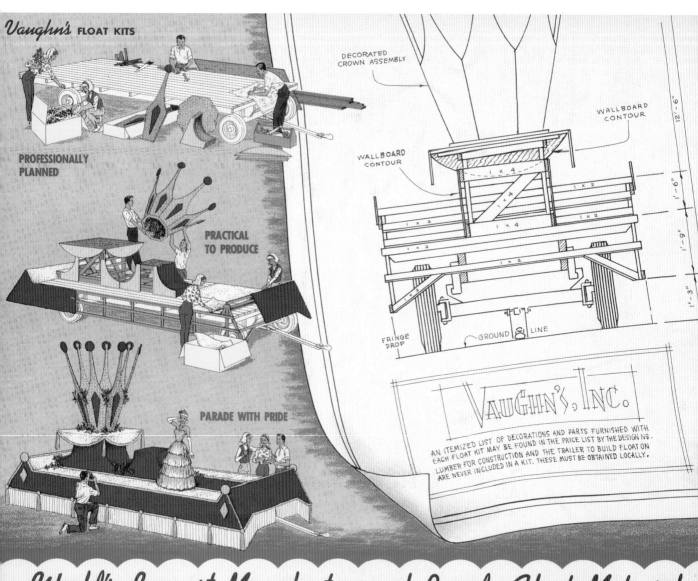

Vaughn's FLOAT KITS

PROFESSIONALLY PLANNED

PRACTICAL TO PRODUCE

PARADE WITH PRIDE

DECORATED CROWN ASSEMBLY

WALLBOARD CONTOUR

WALLBOARD CONTOUR

1 x 4

1 x 2

1 x 2

1 x 2

1 x 4

1 x 2

1 x 2

1 x 2

FRINGE DROP

GROUND LINE

12' - 6"

1' - 6"

1' - 9"

1' - 3"

Vaughn's, Inc.

AN ITEMIZED LIST OF DECORATIONS AND PARTS FURNISHED WITH EACH FLOAT KIT MAY BE FOUND IN THE PRICE LIST BY THE DESIGN N°. LUMBER FOR CONSTRUCTION AND THE TRAILER TO BUILD FLOAT ON ARE NEVER INCLUDED IN A KIT. THESE MUST BE OBTAINED LOCALLY.

World's Largest Manufacturer of Parade Float Materials

universally understood symbol of the good life. In postwar America there was an insatiable appetite for floats, as Vaughn discovered in the prolific work of Herman Smith, who was far and away Vaughn's largest wholesale buyer of float building materials in the early 1950s. From Fargo, North Dakota, Smith developed a topical style that favored scenes of home and family life. A typical scene presented a family at rest under a canopy approximating a well-appointed living room.

In June 1952 Smith staged the Abilene, Kansas, homecoming parade for presidential candidate Dwight David Eisenhower. Smith created twenty-six floats representing notable events in the general's life culminating with a float bearing a beaming likeness of the candidate atop a miniature White House. As the first event of the general's 1952 presidential campaign, the parade and the address that followed were nationally televised. Herman Smith's son Lynn, ten years old at the time, recalled that his family rented a television to watch the parade. Dad of course, was on the scene in Abilene.[36]

Urged by Vaughn, Smith sold his Fargo display service and joined Vaughn's sales department, then shipping crepe paper and float kits to clients by the freight-car load. Lynn Smith, who followed in his father's footsteps and became a display man himself, recalled that his father enjoyed the creative life of a builder. Joining the Vaughn company in his teens, Lynn Smith witnessed the long decline of the float-building business, the bellwether of a changing retail economy of mass markets, and more importantly, distant owners and managements removed from local life and culture. Vaughn, too, was part of the trend. In 1964 Vaughn purchased the legacy businesses of parade and float supply manufacturers John F. Gasthoff and Chicago Artificial Flower. Declining orders for float kits were compensated for with a move into the manufacture of outdoor Christmas decorations for businesses, mostly shopping center parking lots.[37] The float business as Smith's father had known it was dying. "The one time I saw my father cry," Smith recalled, "was at the funeral of a float builder." "I later realized that it wasn't so much for the guy. It was for the scene that was going away."[38]

Before it had gone away, Lynn Smith traveled the country building floats for Parade Productions, a cross-town rival of Vaughn's in Minneapolis. Hitting the road, Smith would often be gone for two, two and a half months at a time. He built floats at the Sun Bowl in El Paso, Texas; the Kentucky Derby in Louisville; and the Tobacco Festival in Richmond, Virginia. Smith did not come off the road until he started a Christmas display business of his own. "It was time," he said, "to live the life for which I had been building floats."

Whether assembled from scratch, from a kit, or by a professional builder who made display a creative livelihood, the float became an icon of community spirit and personal aspiration. Parades that made the transition from local and regional celebrations to nationally televised events enjoyed the advantages of sponsorship. The money was important in staging a spectacle, but in the end, never as important as its reception on the street that welcomed floats with active engagement and affection. Where parades lost their sponsors, participants, and spectators, float construction declined as a symbol of the communities and commercial interests that moved on to other things, complicated by the demands of time, and the alternative ways in which Americans now chose to spend their holidays.

Why Daddy Saves float created by Herman Smith for the First Dakota National Banks, Centennial of Fargo, 1950

CHAPTER 6 : TUDOR TOWN TO TRACT HOME

THE HOLIDAY SETS OF DEPARTMENT STORES in the 1920s were once noted for fanciful Christmas grottoes and live circus acts. By the early 1930s the animals had been replaced by mechanical figures, and the grottoes all but forgotten in a wave of Santa-operated blimps and cruise ships. Yet the theme set with the most staying power was the walk-through village. Wanamaker's *Candy Stick Lane in the Land of Make Believe*, erected in 1927, for example, reflected ideas about the supporting role played by art and architecture in the store's layout and amenities. Marshall Field's *Cozy Cloud Cottage* for another, opened in 1948 as a Chicago home-away-from-home for Santa Claus. The setting incorporated modern design elements that updated the traditional "Santa sits here" approach. As reindeer warmed their hooves around a kitchen stove, in the living room Santa received his young visitors in an armchair instead of a throne.

From the 1920s through the 1960s villages and homes functioned as leading theme sets for Santa and his helpers. To make a space for Santa, department store display men and women initially decorated in the style of the Tudor revival. Adapted for residential use in England and America, the features of Tudor style were decorative half-timbering and cross gables. The style

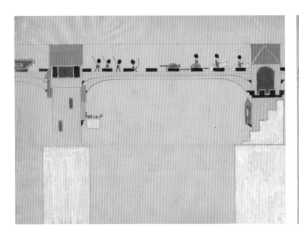

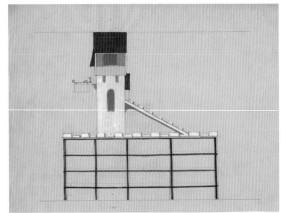
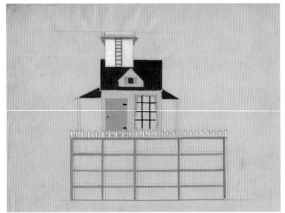

Renderings, toy department displays, Landy R. Hales, date unknown
CLOCKWISE FROM TOP LEFT bridge; drawbridge; house; tower

Macy's Wonderland Village tableau, designed by Landy R. Hales, ca. 1927

appeared as a setting for Santa in England in the 1880s and became popular in America in the 1920s, where it displaced the polar icecap and lighting schemes that likened Santa to the Aurora Borealis.[1] Aside from their use as a cue for Charles Dickens's London since then, Tudor display elements cushioned the presentation of Santa with the charms of "asymmetrical design" and "soft texture."[2] By the 1920s "picturesque" Tudor display elements joined with the "storybook style" of imaginative residential architecture that had begun to appear in Southern California. As described by Arrol Gellner, storybook style was characterized by an "exaggeratedly plastic and often cartoonish

interpretation of medieval forms," featuring stucco finishes, "seawave shingles" and "rolled eves emulating thatch." Like its Tudor cousin, storybook style's picturesque goal was "to elicit an emotional rather than a rational response."[3]

The elements of Tudor and storybook style became popular in Christmas window and toy department displays in the 1920s and 1930s. For example, these display elements became the frame of reference for the commercial artist Harry Taylor, and matrix of Macy's "Wonderland" carried out by puppeteer Tony Sarg and the theatrical designer Landy R. Hales.[4] Though they cannot now be attributed to a specific client, the colorful elevation

Children's souvenir, *Macy's Wonderland*, 1927

Poster study, *Macy's Wonderland*, designed by
Landy R. Hales, 1927

OPPOSITE Macy's toy department, designed by Landy R.
Hales, 1927

plans for toy display settings found in Hales's papers
attest to the popularity of the village theme. Hales
created comparable design elements for Macy's toy
department, complete with streetlamp fixtures that
disguised the load-bearing columns of the building.
Children's souvenirs and posters merchandising
Wonderland carried the idea forward.

The presentation of Santa in a themed display
space naturally suggested more questions than
answers about his likely activities and interests.
Most summoned up the themes of travel and
transportation. At Wanamaker's New York, for
example, Santa appeared in an auditorium stage
show entitled *A Wonderful Trip by Radio Ship*. At
Wanamaker's Philadelphia, Santa appeared as a
kindly village superintendent, receiving children
in front of a shelf of account books indexed by
Philadelphia neighborhood. Completing the
picture of executive ability, the impressive ledgers
presented the jolly old elf as more of an accountant
than a diarist of naughty and nice. Such attention to

Santa with children and ledgers indexed by neighborhood, Wanamaker's Philadelphia, 1926

OPPOSITE Poster, *A Wonderful Trip by Radio Ship* stage show, Wanamaker's Philadelphia, 1926

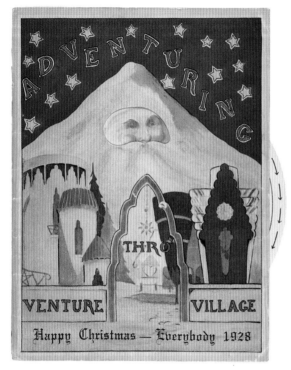

LEFT Children's souvenir booklet, *Thro' Venture Village*, Wanamaker's, Philadelphia, 1928

RIGHT Newspaper advertisement, "On Candy Stick Lane in the Land of Make-Believe," Wanamaker's Philadelphia, 1926

OPPOSITE Construction of *Candy Stick Lane*, Wanamaker's, Philadelphia, 1926

detail tempered the fantasy with a purpose familiar to any retail clerk or manager who compiled names, addresses, and desires for future reference.

John Wanamaker had long championed artistic exhibitions and displays in his stores, a cause embraced by his son Rodman, who took up management of the Philadelphia and New York stores upon his father's death in 1922. Drawing its best promotional ideas from the world of arts and letters, the store distributed colorful illustrated

booklets as a souvenir of a visit to Santa. *Thro' Venture Village*, for example, complemented the spirit of the walk-through story land erected next to the toy department in the store's annex across from the main building. The realization of a village for children and their parents took form in 1926 with the *Candy Stick Lane in the Land of Make Believe*. A special preview invited all of Philadelphia to its evening opening, during which the store was closed and nothing except the idea of visiting the village was sold.

Entrance, *The Land of Really-So*,
Wanamaker's Philadelphia, 1931

The following season the store mounted an "Enchanted Forest" that used chicken wire stretched over wooden forms that provided the basis of tree trunks and archways. If there were any question about the meaning of its *Towne of Make Believe*, they were answered by its playful, yet purposeful location on *Linger Longer Lane*.[5] Though the details changed from year-to-year, the social premise of Wanamaker's storybook "lands" continued unabated. In 1931, for example, the largest display element in *The Land of Really So* was an open book.

The death of Rodman Wanamaker in 1928 was also the passing of the social importance of arts and letters and its relationship to the store. The founder and his son had long sought to integrate the store with the life of the city through the publication of educational tracts, complementary diaries, illustrated city guides with maps, and booklets that described the store's art and architectural features. The impact of Rodman Wanamaker's death was felt by the dealers in paintings, sculpture, and antiques who found their sales offers rejected out of hand by the store's management.[6]

Freed to focus upon the evolution of display, in the postwar era a new generation of specialists extolled the "visual presentations with creative ideas behind them, beautifully designed to sell the store as an institution and to sell merchandise."[7] At holiday time an elaborate light and sound show accompanied by a *Dancing Waters* show appeared in the Grand Court on the mezzanine with the Great Organ. A child-size monorail circled the toy department on a four-hundred-foot track giving riders a birds-eye view of the merchandise displayed below. The genius of the monorail, explained its creator, was the fact that it was suspended from the ceiling, and thus took up no space on the sales floor while giving all a clear view of its wonders.[8]

A similar out-with-the-old, in-with-the-new transition was underway at Marshall Field's in Chicago, where longtime display director Arthur V. Fraser retired in 1944. Fraser's tenure dated to the early enthusiasms of retail showman Harry Selfridge, who had hired Fraser into the Field's fold in 1895. In retirement Fraser outlived his critics, who as early as 1935 had pronounced his mural-type window treatments "stately and dull."[9] Though this view was not widely shared in the profession, by the early 1940s Field's management, anticipating Fraser's retirement, had begun a search for his successor.

The arrival of John Trigg Moss Jr. in 1942 signaled a turning point in the store's design and appearance. Field's vice president for advertising and promotion Lawrence B. Sizer hired Moss to herald the new look of the State Street Leviathan in all its work. A native of St. Louis, Moss graduated from Princeton in 1927, and in 1930 received a Master of Fine Arts in architecture. Employed as an industrial designer by Skidmore, Owings and Merrill, Moss made exhibits for corporate clients at the Chicago Century of Progress and the New York World's Fair. Moss met Sizer, then an N. W. Ayer advertising agency executive, while working on Ford Motor Company's New York World's Fair pavilion.[10]

As Field's director of display and design, Moss fell heir to the traditions of the store's magnanimous public gestures at Christmastime. These included the celebrated Walnut Room restaurant accommodating the largest natural indoor tree in America, decorations for the store's main aisle under two multistoried light wells including the famed Tiffany dome, and thirteen State Street show windows. Taking up residence in the store's thirteenth floor display studio, Moss built a talented staff populated with graduate artists from the Chicago Art Institute and a corps of top tradesmen who were artists in their own right. Sallie Pozniak, an interior designer and recent Art Institute graduate, recalled that the shop's workers were the cream of the crop, hand-picked from other trades within the store.[11] Moss stated that "It is the aim to make all displays either livable or 'lived in,' for display needs to create a feeling in the customers' minds that each item is definitely personal for themselves."[12] This was never more so than at Christmastime, when display suspended disbelief among visitors who became accustomed to seeing enormous snowflakes cascading from the light wells, displays of oversized ornaments and presents on platforms in the store's main aisle, and the Walnut Room's massive fir tree that required the attention of a full-time fireman. Recalling how customers often stopped to watch her and her fellow employees decorate the great tree, Pozniak sighed, "we loved them, and they loved us."[13]

Moss's "new look" for Santa took into account Field's place as a leader among rivals, and a public that expected a spectacle. At first Moss enjoyed success with Clement Moore's *The Night Before Christmas* staged in Field's State Street windows in 1944 and 1945. Sizer had suggested the theme, and in 1946 he suggested another—a Christmas theme that could not be copied by another store, as was done with Moore's poem that had long passed into the public domain.[14] At the time, the most celebrated example of a proprietary character with a story line to boot was Montgomery Ward's *Rudolph the Red-Nosed Reindeer*, created by catalog copy writer Robert L. May. The unassuming May had written the story to read at an office Christmas party. Ward's published the tale in a booklet distributed as a children's souvenir in 1939, and the character's

Toy window magic, Marshall Field & Co., ca. 1951

OPPOSITE Marshall Field main aisle, ca. 1956

Children's souvenir booklet, *Rudolph the Red-Nosed Reindeer*,
Montgomery Ward & Co., 1939

OPPOSITE Reindeer relax in the kitchen, *Cozy Cloud Cottage*,
Marshall Field & Co., 1948

popularity grew with each passing year.[15]

Moss delegated the responsibility for
creating a character, a story, and a window display
to Joanna Osborne, a young stylist and interior
sketch artist. A recent graduate of the Chicago Art
Institute, Osborne's pen and watercolor renderings
of domestic interiors had attracted the attention
of Field's display managers, who offered her a job
in 1943. Asked by Moss to create a "little creature,"
Osborne reflected upon the memory of a beloved
Norwegian Uncle who wore a pork-pie hat. She
described her idea to her husband Addis Osborne, an
artist and Art Institute lecturer, who drew up several
sketches of the character that she thought would
become "Uncle Marshall," a sprightly if somewhat
rotund elf with wings. In conference with Moss and
other executives Osborne's "Uncle Marshall" became
"Uncle Mistletoe."[16]

The Christmas window set introduced Uncle
Mistletoe as Santa Claus's Chicago emissary. The
story was set to verse by Helen McKenna, a store sign
shop artist. Entitled *A Christmas Dream*, McKenna's
verse followed the meter of Clement Moore's *The
Night Before Christmas*. Osborne recalled that she
and McKenna "wanted something else with a
cadence" that viewers "would say to themselves."
The stratagem worked, confirmed by Osborne who
picked up the habit of reading the moving lips of
passersby in front of the window glass.[17]

The first Uncle Mistletoe flew by himself,
though in later treatments he visited the homes
of Chicago children by flying carpet, a feat
understandable given his origin in Field's interior
display studio. In 1947 Osborne and Moss gave him
a wife, "Aunt Holly," and a home, the "Cozy Cloud
Cottage." It was all too easy for Moss, who made a
residence for Uncle Mistletoe, Aunt Holly, and their
guest Santa Claus in the "Modern House," one of
two spacious residential display settings that filled
either end of Field's eighth floor.

In 1947 Moss had outfitted the Modern House
as a furniture showcase for designer T. H. Robsjohn-
Gibbings, who had attracted attention with *Good-
bye, Mr. Chippendale*, a critique of Americans' taste
in antiquities, Tudor towns, mission furniture, and
the Bauhaus. Field's invited Robsjohn-Gibbings

A700

John Moss, floor plan for the living room of the *Cozy Cloud Cottage*, Marshall Field & Co., 1948

OPPOSITE Santa Claus setting with annotations, *Cozy Cloud Cottage*, 1948

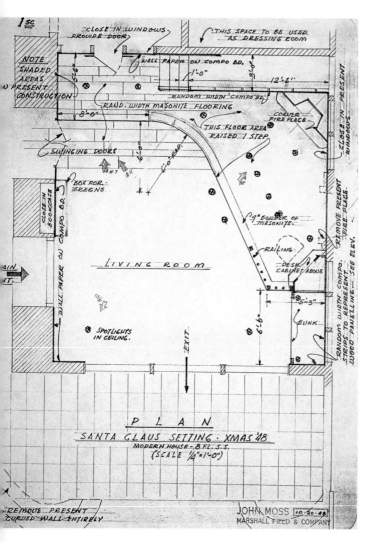

to express his ideas in the Modern House. At the time Robsjohn-Gibbings had just launched a line of modern furnishings with the Widdicomb company of Grand Rapids, Michigan.[18]

It was likely Moss who invited Robsjohn-Gibbings to express his ideas in the Modern House, and it was Moss who turned the concept on its head in refitting the space as the Cozy Cloud Cottage. Visitors waiting to see Santa approached through a baffle-route of tinsel trees, snow, and frolicking animal figures. The kitchen was made over as a parody of the postwar era's good life, with reindeer at rest around a potbelly stove. Visitors greeted Santa in what had been the living room of the future, outfitted with an outdated parlor chair for Santa, and a knock-off Chippendale side chair, neither of which were found in Robsjohn-Gibbings's Widdicomb furniture line.

After a brief conversation with Santa and a pose for the store photographer, visitors followed the rope line out onto a spacious patio, that one year featured a doghouse, and in another, a drive-in snack bar for penguins. Although Robsjohn-Gibbings had every opportunity to visit the Cozy Cloud Cottage, it is not known if he did, or what reaction that he may have had to the improvements introduced over the years, including white icing bedposts, doors with taffy pulls, and cookies that danced on the kitchen's walls.[19] In the early 1970s the baffle-route approach to the Cozy Cloud Cottage enveloped visitors in a remarkable period entertainment of spinning floor-to-ceiling decorations with shiny reflective surfaces. Animated

Penguin drive-in and snack bar, *Cozy Cloud Cottage*, Marshall Field & Co., ca. 1950

OPPOSITE Spinning display elements with static display figures, approach to *Cozy Cloud Cottage*, Marshall Field & Co., ca. 1972

animal figures were replaced by manikins that stood still as the tinseled features twisted all around them.

In the early 1950s Moss played a leading role in the design of Field's new suburban store in Oak Brook, Illinois. Moss used field stone and native materials to fit the store and its outdoor mall to the surrounding landscape. The Modern House remained on exhibit downtown for many years, but was brought back to earth every Christmas by the playful collapse of the traditions of the walk-through display with the "new look" of the stores sprouting in so many places and ways on the outskirts of Chicago. The postwar era's optimism for a suburban design world was first seen downtown in the display world that abandoned Tudor town for the guilty pleasures of a tilted tract home.

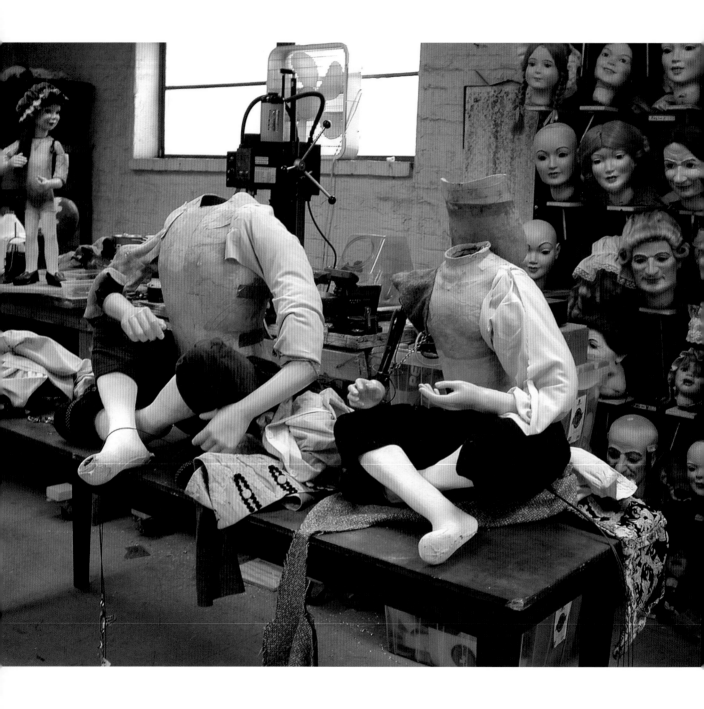

EPILOGUE : WHERE THE STORES WERE

IN 1966 THE DEPARTMENT STORE ECONOMIST noted that the stores that kept "in the forefront of their thinking the idea of a continuing tradition" were leaders beloved by their communities.[1] Riding a short-term wave of prosperity, the nation's department stores were flush with success fueled by suburban expansion. The growth of store chains spurred efforts to distinguish downtown flagship stores from their suburban counterparts. Between Thanksgiving and Christmas they favored animated village displays that were popular among children and adults alike.[2]

The animated village was best experienced in the company of a child, which may only begin to explain its popularity today. Whether in a window or a walk-through setting, the village idea played a reassuring role as the stores of the 1960s began their long decline. So it was more than a shock when many stores retired from business and their traditions too.

The demise of the department store was noted in the museum world, although there was little that anyone seemed to be able to do at the time to collect the passing scene. More than most museums could handle, half- to three-quarter scale storefronts and operating figures posed a nettlesome resource issue. Puzzling out the significance of this miniature animated world was

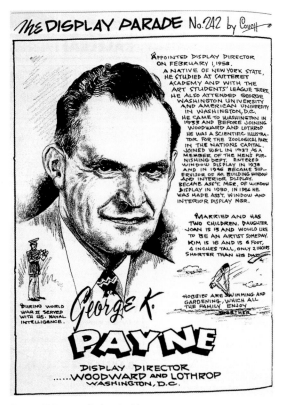

The DISPLAY PARADE No. 242 by Couch

APPOINTED DISPLAY DIRECTOR ON FEBRUARY 1, 1958. A NATIVE OF NEW YORK STATE, HE STUDIED AT CARTERET ACADEMY AND WITH THE ART STUDENTS' LEAGUE THERE. HE ALSO ATTENDED GEORGE WASHINGTON UNIVERSITY AND AMERICAN UNIVERSITY IN WASHINGTON, D.C. HE CAME TO WASHINGTON IN 1933 AND BEFORE JOINING WOODWARD AND LOTHROP HE WAS A SCIENTIFIC ILLUSTRATOR FOR THE ZOOLOGICAL PARK IN THE NATIONS CAPITAL. JOINED W&L IN 1937 AS A MEMBER OF THE MENS FURNISHING DEPT. ENTERED WINDOW DISPLAY IN 1938 AND IN 1946 BECAME SUPERVISOR OF NO. BUILDING WINDOW AND INTERIOR DISPLAY. BECAME ASS'T. MGR. OF WINDOW DISPLAY IN 1950, IN 1956 HE WAS MADE ASS'T. WINDOW AND INTERIOR DISPLAY MGR.

MARRIED AND HAS TWO CHILDREN. DAUGHTER JOAN IS 13 AND WOULD LIKE TO BE AN ARTIST SOMEDAY. KIM IS 16 AND IS 6 FOOT, 4 INCHES TALL, ONLY 2 INCHES SHORTER THAN HIS DAD.

HOBBIES ARE SWIMMING AND GARDENING, WHICH ALL THE FAMILY ENJOY TOGETHER.

DURING WORLD WAR II SERVED WITH U.S. NAVAL INTELLIGENCE.

George K. PAYNE
DISPLAY DIRECTOR
...... WOODWARD AND LOTHROP
WASHINGTON, D.C.

George K Payne, *Display World*, 1959

all the more problematic because its popularity with the public seemed a world unto its own. On the other hand, there was little doubt about the imaginative quality of the work and the competitive environment of stores that had once placed a great deal of emphasis upon holiday display.

At the time that they closed, two stores were in possession of "Enchanted Village" attractions made by Germany's Christian Hofmann Company. A two-hundred-year-old toy firm located in Bad Rodach, Germany, Christian Hoffman's clients included Washington, D.C.'s Woodward & Lothrop,

New York's Stern Brothers, Philadelphia's Lit Brothers, and Boston's Jordan Marsh. Portions of Lit Brothers' *Enchanted Christmas Village* may be visited between Thanksgiving and New Years Day at the Please Touch Museum, the children's museum of Philadelphia. The former Jordan Marsh "Enchanted Village" is exhibited annually by the Mayor and City of Boston.[3]

The creation of animated figures and displays in Germany held considerable appeal for American department store display managers. Christian Hofmann's work offered a high level of craftsmanship, a favorable exchange rate, and the opportunity to travel to its Bad Rodach workshop to pantomime the desired figure movements. Their entertaining scenes and settings were extremely popular with the public. Woodward & Lothrop's *A Window on Williamsburg*, for example, featured one hundred Christian Hofmann figures in eight window display settings. George K. Payne, Woodies' vice president for display, designed the detailed architectural scenic backgrounds built by the craftsmen of the store's display shop. The show opened to great acclaim Thanksgiving Day 1966 and ran through the first week of January 1967. The display became so popular that it attracted an average of fifty thousand visitors per day, an audience surpassing the combined daily attendance of Smithsonian museums.[4]

Payne's method may be regarded as typical of the time. Holiday display burnished the reputation of the locally owned and operated department store, where free rein was given to the display

Animated Three Bears window display, Woodward & Lothrop, 1951

manager, a topic that Payne expounded upon at length in his 1965 book entitled *Creative Display*. The store's management believed that its public thirsted for displays that made the downtown shopping district the place to be. Animated displays became the stuff of family outings, a special occasion for leisure and shopping that reflected the store's identity as a retail institution.[5]

Previously Payne had purchased animated units on the secondary market in New York. Roland Leimbach, a former Woodward & Lothrop vice president for display who had once worked for Payne, recalled that Payne's practice was to purchase a year-old Bliss Display window set for about thirty thousand dollars, use it for two years, sell it to a down-market store, and buy a different set, amortizing expenses while keeping current with the best in holiday display.[6]

In 1957 Payne set out to build an animated window set unique to his store. Presented in 1959, the display featured an animated Victorian "cat city" set in 1880, the year that Woodward & Lothrop had opened. Store craftsmen built the scenic backgrounds; Christian Hofmann made the animated figures. Payne conceived the idea of having the figures made in Germany first, and the idea of cats later, because he found that Christian Hofmann's figures were "too scary for little children, with funny old gnomes and long beards."[7] Payne noted that when Christian Hofmann's figures arrived from Germany they had to be "fattened up" with "a little extra stuffing" as a concession to American tastes —no small consideration at holiday time.[8]

Colonial figures and historical settings for *A Window on Williamsburg* playfully expanded upon the method of Colonial Williamsburg's carefully restored buildings and costumed interpreters.[9] As a reproduction of a restoration, the show's extraordinary attention to detail contributed to its charming effect. Store craftsmen rendered large corner window settings depicting Bruton Parish Church and the Governor's Palace with forced perspective techniques that heightened the perception of depth. They counted and faithfully reproduced the number of bricks on building exteriors and recreated in miniature the moldings in the Palace supper room and scaled-down wallpapers. Ever mindful of historical detail, the display did not include Christmas trees or Santa Claus. For the benefit of a wondering public a store press release explained that Christmas trees, like Santa, were "historically absent."[10]

Before it had completed its holiday run A Window on Williamsburg was sold to a wax museum

planning to open on the outskirts of Williamsburg, Virginia. The Colonial Williamsburg Foundation intervened with Woodward & Lothrop to void the wax museum's sales contract, setting off a heated discussion about the appropriate place of the display and the power of animated displays as a tourist draw. Foundation officials argued that they had given the store permission to make the display and had lent their expertise to help create it. The fact that it would be exhibited by a wax museum in the orbit of Colonial Williamsburg was simply unacceptable.[11] After a lengthy negotiation, Williamsburg Restoration, the foundation's commercial arm, agreed to purchase it from Woodward & Lothrop for twenty thousand dollars. Whether or not the store recouped its settlement with the wax museum for breaking its contract is not clear.[12]

The extraordinary effort launched by Colonial Williamsburg Foundation officials to overturn the sale of *A Window on Williamsburg* was a perverse testimonial of its power. The controversy raised questions about the boundaries between museums, stores, and destination tourism, subjects very much on the mind of foundation officials. Immediately after taking possession of the display in 1969, the newly reorganized Williamsburg Restoration rented it for the season to Richmond, Virginia's Miller & Rhoads department store.[13] The Restoration quickly reclaimed a portion of its twenty thousand dollar purchase price and perhaps grasped the ways in which its popular appeal transcended commercial considerations, a point that Payne and the wax museum's proprietors understood implicitly.

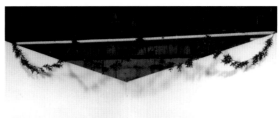

Wig shop, animated window settings set up for a trial run at Woodward & Lothrop's service building, Washington, D.C., 1966

OPPOSITE TOP Williamsburg Governor's Palace, Woodward & Lothrop, 1966

OPPOSITE BOTTOM Wythe house parlor and staircase, Woodward & Lothrop, 1966

Christmas catalog cover featuring Lit Brothers Enchanted Christmas Village, Philadelphia, 1963

OPPOSITE, CLOCKWISE FROM TOP LEFT Entrance to Lit Brothers' Enchanted Christmas Village; animated Schoolroom; three-quarter-scale figures; animated blacksmith setting, Lit Brothers, Philadelphia, 1966

In later years, the managers of Merchants Square, the Restoration's tourist shopping district near Williamsburg's interpretive city center, found ready use for Christian Hofmann's figures and Payne's scenic architectural elements. The elements were cut down, not without irony, to fit Merchants Square's demure colonial storefronts.[14] After that, Woodward & Lothrop's Roland Leimbach recalled borrowing figures and settings for the store's 1980 centenary celebration and then returning them to Williamsburg. Though the figures and settings cannot be located today, there is reason to believe that they fell apart from wear and tear and were thrown away.

Where holiday displays were recovered and exhibited, the first steps to be taken usually were not by a museum or a store, but by the individuals who remembered them most. This was the case in Philadelphia, where the on-again off-again afterlife of Lit Brothers' *Enchanted Christmas Village* began when the store abruptly closed in 1977. Unlike *A Window on Williamsburg*, which was exhibited but a single holiday season, Lit Brothers' Enchanted Christmas Village had built a reservoir of holiday memory among the estimated ten million Philadelphians and out-of-town guests who visited the display between 1962 and 1976. Lit Brothers vice president for display Thomas Comerford conceived the village as a response to the holiday attractions mounted by its Market Street rivals Gimbels, Strawbridge & Clothier, and Wanamaker's. Like Woodies' George Payne, Comerford too had made the pilgrimage to Christian Hofmann's Bad Rodach workshop in 1961, commissioning the

Enchanted Christmas Village for an amount just under $27,000.[15] Christian Hofmann furnished the display in its entirety, complete with three-quarter-scale colonial-themed shops, homes, and animated costumed figures. The scenes included a bakery, watchmaker, village store, tailor shop, wigmaker, butcher, candle-maker, glassblower, toy maker, candy shop, shoemaker, blacksmith shop, an inn, and a school. The last scene was a comfortable home in which a family gathered for a holiday meal.

The village square became a space for "creative display features" such as "dancing, cavorting, sky-larking animals," ice skaters, and a sleigh with a swish-tail pony. At least one wag pointed out that colonial Quaker society did not celebrate Christmas. Comerford replied that historical accuracy was not the point. The concept, he explained, "is a blending of the colonial village with all that children dream of at Christmas." Contributing to the display's longevity, Comerford and company never had to dismantle it for storage. After New Year's they simply closed it off in a wing of the store on the second floor beyond the toy department. They refurbished it at their leisure and reopened it every Thanksgiving.[16]

The promotion of Lit Brothers as a retail institution endeared the Enchanted Christmas Village to Philadelphians of all ages and walks of life. The annual ribbon-cutting ceremony featured the mayor of Philadelphia and the city's superintendent of schools. The store lavished special attention upon visiting school groups with scheduled viewing appointments. The expansive layout of the village

made it a truly enchanting place. Gerald Lamparter, whose photographs captured the display at the height of its powers in 1966, noted that animated figures and features tucked into every corner of the display charmed adults, who were often seen wandering through it unaccompanied by children.[17]

When Lit Brothers filed for bankruptcy protection in 1977, the outpouring of memories commenced, and the search for a local display venue began. What followed can only be described as the most convoluted chain of possession in the modern history of display. Determined that the Enchanted Christmas Village remain in Philadelphia, the Sun Oil Company (Sunoco) purchased it at Lit Brothers' liquidation sale for thirty-five thousand dollars. Sun Oil executives hoped that the City of Philadelphia might take it, but, for lack of a suitable place in which to store and show it, the city did not. Thus began the display's odyssey from Longwood Gardens at Kennett Square, Pennsylvania, to the Smithsonian Institution's Office of Horticulture, back to the former Lit Brothers building under the auspices of the Atwater Kent Museum, and finally to the Please Touch Museum. Each stage of the village's development as an exhibition raised questions about its cultural significance, that in most cases were overridden by its personal meaning.

Presented under the auspices of the Smithsonian and the Atwater Kent, the reappearance of the Enchanted Christmas Village as an exhibit in City Center Philadelphia in November 1988 was welcomed by Philadelphians as if it were the magical disappearing and reappearing village

"Brigadoon." On opening day some two hundred parents, grandparents, teenagers, and toddlers lined the exhibit entrance at Mellon Independence Center, the retail-office shopping complex that now occupied the former Lit Brothers building. Children who had grown up since the display's last appearance at Longwood Gardens in the late 1970s stood in line, at one with the sentiment of its cleverly titled advertising campaign, "Give your kids a holiday you remember."

Museum volunteers urged visitors to sign a petition asking the Atwater Kent to negotiate with the Smithsonian to convert its loan to a gift. Atwater Kent Museum director John V. Alviti later explained to the somewhat perturbed Smithsonian Office of Horticulture director James R. Buckler that "the spirit of the petition was not adversarial.... If that opportunity [to evaluate the public's perception of the Village as a cultural treasure] was not present, then the entire project would be little more than a sentimental publicity scheme, something in which the Atwater Kent Museum would not be interested in participating."[18]

Despite Alviti's unsentimental intent, the visitors who flocked to the exhibition were demonstrably sentimental about it. Manning a table stacked with Atwater Kent's petitions to the Smithsonian, sisters Molly and Ana Adams recalled annual visits to the village with their mother, "hands clasped as they oohed and ahhed, gawked and dragged their feet when it was time to go." And their expectations today? "We want it back here, where it belongs."[19]

As the Enchanted Christmas Village finished the season as an exhibit in a Center City shopping mall, its popular reception helped set in motion its de-accession by the Smithsonian. Like Longwood Gardens before it, the Smithsonian's Office of Horticulture decided to refocus its resources on plant specimen and garden collections, rather than animated displays. Buckler, too, retired and moved on to other things. Preparing the de-accession request, Horticulture's Kathryn Meehan noted the original impetus behind its accession. Acknowledging Atwater Kent's petition drive, Meehan concluded, "A new generation of Philadelphians has been born since the original displays and unquestionably a proprietary interest exists in this unique tradition come home."[20]

After reviewing the prospects for the village's exhibition and long-term care, Smithsonian officials formally donated it to the Atwater Kent Museum in 1991. Atwater Kent exhibited seven of the animated storefront scenes that could be made to work until 1994, and quietly warehoused the village in surplus city property. So powerful was its appeal, however, that in 2000 the village was rescued from a leaky Philadelphia firehouse by the Please Touch Museum with an $845,000 grant from the Philadelphia Foundation to restore the display to working order.

In its current state, the Enchanted Christmas Village is not thought of as a commercial display or as an inviolable museum artifact; but rather as an operating, changing annual exhibition, not unlike a holiday display in a department store, which is the point. As a condition of its restoration, the Please

Touch Museum has introduced new figures of color in a bid for contemporary social relevance. Coming into possession in 2001, museum specialists performed a comprehensive assessment of the figures and settings that laid a foundation for a plan of mechanical and aesthetic restoration, one storefront at a time.[21] Bouyed by memory, the Enchanted Colonial Village has been discovered by the children of the children who first stood in awe of its powers.

The sentimental attachment to holiday display had always played a part in the reception of settings like *A Window on Williamsburg* and the *Enchanted Colonial Village*. In their half- and three-quarter-scale storefronts resided what many viewers regarded as ultimate, if quite fantastic walking around towns that turned the gritty reality of the center city into a memorable experience that took seriously the value of the village within.

The closure of retailers like Lit Brothers and Woodward & Lothrop left cities with emotional spaces to fill. For some, an answer was found not in the return of a central store, but in concentrations of cultural attractions such as aquariums, science centers, festival marketplaces, and the display of mall-style, limited animation figures at holiday time. Of the downtown stores that remain today, the economics of distant ownership colors the commitment to creative display. Most have learned that in matters of customer loyalty, they can no sooner quit the traditions of holiday display than go out of business, but that has happened.

In the last days of Washington, D.C.'s Woodward & Lothrop, the store decorated for Christmas in October. A red paper handbill with a silhouette of a Christmas tree spiked with a jack-o-lantern explained, "Since Woodies will be closing in just a few weeks, we won't be sharing the holidays together. Many of you asked to see our famous traditional Christmas one last time, and to thank you for your loyalty, we're celebrating a little bit early this year!" Shoppers perused the store's main aisle, strewn with cast-off merchandise and boxes of business records. Disbelieving shoppers followed in the wake of the store's liquidation. As a former saleswoman put it, "I always thought that I'd go bankrupt before they did."[22]

Like the periodic clean-out of antiquated display props, a new round of retail consolidation had just begun. Becoming part of a retail chain was no guarantee of longevity, as the boarded up buildings of the downtown retail core testified. The display companies, whose props, features, and effects had once bedazzled viewers, moved on too. The business of the Messmore & Damon Company migrated to theatrical sets for feature films and television soap operas, while a new business incorporated in 1981 produced cardiology patient simulators used to train physicians in diagnosing the symptoms of heart disease.

With continuing television sponsorship, the Macy's Thanksgiving Day Parade and Pasadena's Tournament of Roses achieved their highest ratings in the late 1960s and early 1970s, propelled by the novelty of color television and the limited viewing choices offered by three national television networks. The Tournament of Roses became an

TOP Pocketbook float illustrating the "Famous Books" parade theme, Tournament of Roses, Pasadena, 1954

BOTTOM A precision drill team of unknown shoppers per–form in the fourth annual Doo Dah Parade, Pasadena, 1981

object of parody in the 1990s with the untelevised post–Thanksgiving Day "Doo Dah" parade on Colorado Street. The Tournament had once been open to the kind of self-parody that turned the parade theme into a play on words. A 1956 "pocketbook" float, for example, became *Our Favorite Book*. The Doo Dah parade featured drill teams of wheezing lawn mower operators and shopping cart shoppers wearing brown paper bags over their heads. For lack of television sponsorship, Miami's Orange Bowl Committee ended the long run of the King Orange Festival Parade in 2001.

Among the beneficiaries of suburban growth, Vaughn Displays turned from making parade supplies and float kits to the manufacture of outdoor Christmas decorations. Vaughn's enormous electrical display fixtures were purchased by some downtown business improvement districts, though Vaughn found that they were mostly purchased to enliven the light posts of shopping mall parking lots. Vaughn and its West Coast rival Valley Decorating Company (who also refocused its manufacturing operations on Christmas décor) experienced disruptions caused by energy conservation concerns in 1973 that made holiday lighting a symbol of unwelcome extravagance. Cooler heads prevailed, and by 1974 the decorations began to come back in the name of tradition and efficient low-watt lamp engineering.

The animated display window was not as fortunate. The imperatives of visual merchandising dictated that display focus its energies at the point of sale, thus diminishing the role of windows in

35' Chandelier with 3½' vinyl star   *50' Vertical Tree with 3½' vinyl star*

Give sizes and complete installation
hardware are included with every
crank-up spectacular decoration. All
are packed and shipped in heavy-duty

cases for protection and between
season storage. Instructions are carefully illustrated with step-by-step
installation explanations.

35' CHANDELIER	50' CHANDELIER	35' VERTICAL TREE	50' VERTICAL TREE
Garland optional	Garland optional	Garland optional	Garland optional
4' vinyl star & six	5' vinyl star & eight	4' vinyl star	5' vinyl star
6' red candles	6' red candles		
4220 watts / 931 lbs	7300 watts / 1915 lbs	4160 watts / 610 lbs	7600 watts / 1865 lbs
ORDER: No. 143-50	ORDER: No. 143-51	ORDER: No. 143-08	ORDER: No. 143-09
PRICE: $2,360.00	PRICE: $3,995.00	PRICE: $2,895.00	PRICE: $4,490.00

All decorations on this page are available in your choice of Super Sheen, Color
Blend or Silver Blend garlands (see pages 2 & 3). When ordering, please specify
color choice & type of garland.

31

WHY VALLEY DECORATIONS ARE CALLED ''THE SELF-INSTALLABLES''

A. SPACE-SAVING DESIGN
The Spiral tree shown here is pre-assembled and shipped in a
strong storage box. This is typical of the thoroughness in
pre-assembly and compact packaging in all Valley decorations.
Saves valuable storage space between seasons too!

B. SELF-STANDING DECORATIONS
The special Valley engineered "crank-up" allows quick erection of all
self-standing spectaculars.

C. POLE DECORATIONS
Everything necessary for installation is included in the price of
each pole decoration. Install faceplate, insert decoration — plug in.
Faceplates may be left on pole year after year.

D. BUILDING FRONT DECORATIONS
Building front decorations are shipped pre-assembled, ready for
installation. Included in price are hanging cables, tiedown cords,
and 20' long electric lead-in wire. New for 1970 is the hanger
bracket. Specify thickness of parapet wall (see "E" dimension in
illustration).

E. CRANK-UP TOWERS
The heart of all crank-up spectaculars, their towers cut installation
time in half.

All Valley decorations are packed with simple fully illustrated
installation directions. They clearly spell out all that you need to
know to be a "self-installable" expert.

NOTE: Constant product testing and improvement at Valley assures our customers of the highest quality in the industry.

40

TOP Trade catalog picturing "giant crank-up spectacular" decorations for shopping centers, Valley Decorating Company, 1970

BOTTOM Joan Benjamin of Spaeth Design preparing animated figures for Lord & Taylor, 1984

general. The tradition of the animated holiday display could be found in pockets in New York along Fifth Avenue and Broadway and in Chicago on State Street. For the writers and social critics who sought them out, the windows provided a nostalgic puff of whimsy, humor, and fantasy on the cold sidewalks of the walking around town, an experience best "savored on foot…with a clutch of hot chestnuts in the pocket for warmth."[23]

The chilly prospects for the future of display could be read in the trend toward "shopping intensification," the logical culmination of a culture that produced consumers as efficiently as it produced goods. This was not necessarily a new idea, but rather the fruition of an old one that informed the inward-looking appearance of the suburban shopping mall. Though not unique to the mall, the trend of intensification picked up speed with merchandising concepts that enticed consumers with barrier-free shopping.[24] While the mall acknowledged the old amenities to a point, its unencumbered sightlines emphasized the merchandise more. For example, architect Victor Gruen, who designed the first enclosed mall in the United States in suburban Minneapolis in 1955, anchored his projects with a department store fronted with a public gathering space.[25] At Christmastime, it became a ceremonial space for great trees and ornamental features mounted by a centralized mall management—but not so great that the features detracted from the merchandising responsibilities of the mall tenant.

No longer did store display managers put time and attention into animated features. That level of energy was demanded elsewhere in the store. James Albert Bliss, who had coined the expression "visual merchandising" while championing the kind of animated features that had once been the pride of individual store owners and their display managers, found that such amenities had gone the way of the downtown store. In the late 1970s Bliss's business no longer specialized in display, but display *brackets* for shoes and apparel that had become the mainstays of open-shelf retailing.[26]

As developers looked to Gruen's and other's plans for their own shopping centers, Gruen noted that only the most profitable features were ever copied, implying that the community-oriented features of his original plan were not.[27] This reductive process came to include a single feature such as a tree, accompanied by a fence-lined route into a display setting for Santa. Decorative touches incorporating festoons and garlands apportioned throughout the mall and its parking lots completed the picture for most shoppers.

By the 1990s the phenomenon of retail intensification had left in its wake a hierarchy of mall types, lead by the "power mall," a collection of "category killer" stores. In hindsight the ritual stripping away of display made the attributes of the traditional mall look great in comparison.[28] Yet another retail tradition had been consigned to the museum of lost amenities, removed from the idle charms of the walking around town.

A round-table forum for Santa Clauses sponsored by *Parents Magazine*, 1948

NOTES

ABBREVIATIONS USED IN NOTES

AC/NMAH	Archives Center, National Museum of American History
CWF	Colonial Williamsburg Foundation
DW	*Display World*
HSP	Historical Society of Pennsylvania
MR&SW	*Merchants Record and Show Window*
NP	Nela Park
NYT	*New York Times*
OH/SI	Office of Horticulture, Smithsonian Institution
PTM	Please Touch Museum
P&R/NMAH	Division of Politics and Reform, National Museum of American History
SW	*Show Window*

INTRODUCTION

1. Eric Hobsbawm, "The Invention of Tradition," and "Mass Producing Traditions, 1870–1914," in *The Invention of Tradition*, ed. Hobsbawm and Terence Ranger, (Cambridge: Cambridge University Press, 1982), 1–14, 263–307; J.M. Bowden, "The Invention of American Tradition," *Journal of Historical Geography* 18 (1992): 3–26; Susan G. Davis, *Parades and Power: Street Theatre in Nineteenth-Century Philadelphia* (Berkeley, Calif.: University of California Press, 1986); Ellen M. Litwicki, *America's Public Holidays, 1865–1920* (Washington, D.C.: Smithsonian Institution Press, 2000); Brooks McNamara, *Day of Jubilee: The Great Age of Public Celebrations in New York, 1788–1909* (New Brunswick, N.J.: Rutgers University Press, 1997); Thomas M. Spencer, *The St. Louis Veiled Prophet Celebration: Power on Parade, 1877–1995* (Columbia, Mo.: University of Missouri Press, 2000); William B. Waits, *The Modern Christmas in America: A Cultural History of Gift Giving* (New York: New York University Press, 1993); Penne L. Restad, *Christmas in America: A History* (New York: Oxford University Press, 1995); Stephen Nissenbaum, *The Battle for Christmas* (New York: Alfred A. Knopf, 1996). For the exceptions that weigh the emotional complexities of holiday display, see Karal Ann Marling, *Merry Christmas! Celebrating America's Greatest Holiday* (Cambridge, Mass.: Harvard University Press, 2000); Jack Elliott, *Inventing Christmas: How Our Holiday Came to Be* (New York: H. N. Abrams, 2002); and Leigh Eric Schmidt, *Consumer Rites: The Buying and Selling of American Holidays* (Princeton, N.J.: Princeton University Press, 1995).
2. David Glassberg, *American Historical Pageantry: The Uses of Tradition in the Early Twentieth Century* (Chapel Hill, N.C.: University of North Carolina Press, 1990); Naima Prevots, *American Pageantry: A Movement for Art & Democracy* (Ann Arbor, Mich.: UMI Research Press, 1990); Neil Harris, "Museums, Merchandising and Popular Taste: The Struggle for Influence," in *Cultural Excursions: Marketing Appetites and Cultural Tastes in Modern America*, ed. Harris (Chicago: University of Chicago Press, 1990), 56–81; William Leach, *Land of Desire: Merchants, Power, and the Rise of a New American Culture* (New York: Pantheon, 1993); Leach, "Strategists of Display and the Production of Desire," in *Consuming Visions: Accumulation and Display of Goods in America, 1880–1920*, ed. Simon Bronner (New York: W. W. Norton & Co., 1989), 99–132; Bill Lancaster, *The Department Store: A Social History* (London: Leicester University Press, 1995); Sarah Elvins, *Sales & Celebrations: Retailing and Regional Identity in Western New York State, 1920–1940* (Athens, Ohio: Ohio University Press, 2004), 155.

CHAPTER ONE

1. Harry Harman, *Christmas Displays* (Louisville, Ky.: Harry Harman, 1890), Library of Congress.
2. Editorial, "The Age of Progress," *The Show Window* [hereafter SW] 4, (January 1899): 1.
3. *SW* 5 (November 1899): 205.
4. Frank L. Carr, Jr., *The Wide-Awake Window Dresser* (New York: Dry Goods Economist, 1894), 5.
5. Rudolph Stritt, "Window Trimming a Business Art," *SW* 6 (15 April 1900): 202–6.
6. Jerome A. Koerber, "After Hours," *Merchants Record and Show Window* [hereafter MR&SW] 33 (August 1913): 13–14. Koerber's Christmas installations are featured in *One Hundred Good Holiday Displays* (Chicago: Merchants Record Company, 1913).
7. "Special Street Fair Edition," *SW* 6 (15 April 1900).
8. "Floral Parades," *MR&SW* 34 (May 1914): 40–41; "Floral Parades," 32 (May 1913): 35; (May 1913): 38–39; 36 (May 1915): 16–18.
9. Ad, J. F. Gasthoff, *MR&SW* 46 (April 1920):4; 46 (May 1920): 4; trade catalog, Gasthoff's Manufacturing Company, Inc., "Gasthoff's Parade Floats and Decorations, 1937–1938"; "Schack's Floral Parade Book," *MR&SW* 32 (May 1913): 54; obituary, "Death of Ludolf Bauman," *MR&SW* 34 (March 1914): 36.
10. Ad, Joseph Schack, *MR&SW* 46 (May 1920): 11.
11. Earl Hargrove, interview, Landover, Md., June 12, 2002; Lynn Smith, interview, Golden Valley, Minn., 26 April 2002.
12. "The Canadian Convention," *MR&SW* 35 (September 1914): 50.
13. John H. Meyer, "To Attract Attention," *New York Times* [hereafter NYT], 28 August 1921.
14. Julius Schneider, "Cooperation in Display," *MR&SW* 35 (September 1914): 36–37.
15. A. W. Lindblom, "Say 'Display Man,'" *MR&SW* 35 (November 1914): 58.
16. *The Koester School Year Book* (Chicago: The Koester School, n.d.).
17. Ad, Harry Taylor, *MR&SW* 61 (August 1927): 4.
18. "Bliss in Expansion Move," *Display World* [hereafter DW] 64 (March 1954): 40–41.
19. Fleur Fenton, "World Trip of Yuletide in Windows," (1933), pasted in scrapbook, Landy R. Hales papers, collection 906, Archive Center, National Museum of American History, [hereafter AC/NMAH].

CHAPTER TWO

1. "Holiday Trade," *NYT*, 15 December 1870.
2. Ibid.; "R. H. Macy & Co.," *NYT*, 15 December 1874; Ralph M. Hower, *History of Macy's of New York, 1858–1919: Chapters in the Evolution of the Department Store* (Cambridge, Mass.: Harvard University Press, 1943), 118.
3. Knickerbocker, "Notes from New York," *SW* 9 (December 1901): 226; 10 (January 1902): 18.
4. Edward Hungerford, *The Romance of a Great Store* (New York: Robert M. McBride & Company, 1922), 17, 43–44; "Holiday Tableaus: The Display that Is Being Prepared by R. H. Macy & Co.," *NYT* 16 November 1889, 8. Creating figures for sale or lease for advertising purposes appears to have arrived as a marketable Musée function in the 1890s. Ad, Eden Musée, "Correct Reproduction of Subjects and Groups in Wax," *Monthly Catalogue* (September 1896), 28.
5. "Chicago's Holiday Windows," *SW* 7 (15 December 1900): 249.
6. Joseph Arrington, "John Maelzel, Master Showman of Automata and Panoramas," *Pennsylvania Magazine of History and Biography* 84 (January 1960): 56–92; Michael O'Malley and Carlene E. Stephens, "Clockwork History: Monumental Clocks and the Depiction of the American Past," *National Association of Watch and Clock Collectors Bulletin* 32 (February 1990): 3–15; On Barnum's enthusiasm for animated novelties see Phineas T. Barnum, *The Colossal P. T. Barnum Reader: Nothing Else Like It in the Universe,* ed. James W. Cook (Urbana, Ill.: University of Illinois Press, 2005), 71; Gaby Wood, *Edison's Eve: A Magical History of the Quest for Mechanical Life* (New York: Alfred A. Knopf, 2002), 75–76, 217; Neil Harris, *Humbug: The Art of P. T. Barnum* (Boston: Little, Brown & Co., 1973), 59–90.
7. "The Ehrich Brothers' Circus," *NYT*, 27 November 1881, 7.
8. Hower, *History of Macy's of New York, 1858–1919,* 169; *Frank Leslie's Illustrated Newspaper,* 20 December 1884, reproduced in ad, "Macy's Red Star Express," *NYT* 24 November 1923, 5; Phillip Snyder, *December 25th The Joys of Christmas Past* (New York: Dodd, Mead & Company, 1985), 88–89; Marling, *Merry Christmas!* 87–90.
9. Hower, *History of Macy's of New York, 1858–1919,* 461, note 22.
10. Editorial, "The Age of Progress," *SW* 4 (January 1899): 1; *SW* 5 (November 1899): 209.
11. Baum, "Business Windows," *SW* 5 (September 1899): 139–41; "Charles W. Morton," *MR&SW* 44 (February 1919): 48.
12. F. F. Purdy, "Notes from New York," *MR&SW* 47 (December 1920): 18–23; Edward N. Goldsman, "London Display Topics," *MR&SW* 66 (January 1930): 46–50. Lancaster, *The Department Store,* 22–23, 26, 51; Mark Connely, *Christmas: A Social History* (New York: St. Martin's Press, 1999), 192–93.
13. Lancaster, *The Department Store,* 3–4, 16–19; Leach, *Land of Desire,* 81–84; Harris, "Museums, Merchandising and Popular Taste;" Susan Porter Benson, *Counter Cultures: Saleswomen, Managers, and Customers in American Department Stores, 1890–1940* (Urbana, Ill.: University of Illinois Press, 1986), 19–20; John Henry Hepp IV, *The Middle-Class City: Transforming Space and Time in Philadelphia, 1876–1926* (Philadelphia: University of Pennsylvania Press, 2003), 144–48.
14. John William Ferry, *A History of the Department Store* (New York: Macmillan, 1960), 38–39; Harris, "Museums, Merchandising and Popular Taste."
15. F. F. Purdy, "Notes from New York," *MR&SW* 34 (February 1914): 36–40; Leonard S. Marcus, *The American Store Window* (New York: Whitney Library of Design, 1978), 66.
16. Robert P. Lederman, *Christmas on State Street: 1940s and Beyond* (Chicago: Arcadia Publishing, 2002); Benson, *Counter Cultures,* 14.
17. Kresge Department Store, formerly L. S. Plaut & Co., Newark, N.J., *Santa's Own Storybook,* n.d.
18. Marshall Field & Company, paper novelty treasure chest, 1925.
19. "Chicago Toy Displays," *MR&SW* 33 (October 1913): 40–43.
20. John Wanamaker, *Golden Book of the Wanamaker Stores* (Philadelphia, Pa.: John Wanamaker, 1911), 81.
21. Stewart passed away in 1876 and the business left to his management "fell away." Ferry, *A History of the Department Store,* 43.
22. On Stewart's influence see Herbert Ershkowitz, *John Wanamaker: Philadelphia Merchant* (Conshocken, Pa.: Combined Publishing, 1999), 109; Joseph H. Appel, *The Business Biography of John Wanamaker, Founder and Builder* (New York: AMS Press, 1930), 122–23; Herbert Adams Gibbons, *John Wanamaker* vol. two (Port Washington, N.Y.: Kennikat Press, 1926), 5–13.
23. Purdy, "Notes from New York," *MR&SW* 47 (December 1920): 18–23 and 48 (January 1921): 27–32.
24. "Macy's, the Christmas Store," *Sparks* (December 1925): 1–2; Purdy, "Notes form New York," *MR&SW* 32 (January 1913): 46.
25. Purdy, "Notes from New York," *MR&SW* 53 (December 1923): 13–18.
26. Grover A. Whalen, *Mr. New York: The Autobiography of Grover A. Whalen* (New York: G. P. Putnam's Sons, 1955), 93–94, 104–31, 167–68; Geoffrey T. Hellman, "Profiles: For City and for Coty–1," *New Yorker* 27 (14 July 1951): 28–45; Purdy, "Notes from New York," *MR&SW* 61 (July 1927): 32–34; "Tercentenary," *New Yorker* 1 (24 October 1925): 5–6.
27. "Boom Christmas Business," *MR&SW* 51 (October 1922): 39–40.

CHAPTER THREE

1. The first notices of Johnson's efforts appeared in the *Detroit Post and Tribune,* 1892, and "In and About the City: A Brilliant Christmas Tree: How an Electrician Amused His Children," *NYT,* 27 December 1884, both cited in George Nelson, "A Brief History of Electrical Christmas Lighting in America," http://www.oldchristmaslights.com/history.htm.
2. "A Tune in Colors: A Novel Feature of the Foreign Fair—A Christmas Tree with Electrical Decorations," *Boston Daily Globe,* 20 December 1883; for passing mention of the electrical Christmas tree mounted by New York's Eden Musée see "Notes of the Week," *NYT,* 28 December 1884; "Yuletide Tableaux: Germania Club's Beautiful Celebration of Christmas," *Chicago Daily,* 27 December 1891; "Tree that Grows Coin: the Costliest Christmas Celebration in America," *Washington Post,* 21 December 1896, 8.
3. Ivan E. Houk, "Yule Lighting in Denver," *Light* (December 1924): 11, 44; "Middlebury Sends Tree to Coolidge, College's Gift Will Be Erected Near the White House as 'National Christmas Tree,'" *NYT,* 13 December 1923, 21; "White House Carols and Brilliant Tree Usher in Christmas," *Washington Post,* 25 December 1923, 1; John A. Jakle, *City Lights: Illuminating the American Night* (Baltimore, Md.: Johns Hopkins University Press, 2001), 139–41.
4. "'Electrical Shrubbery'—A Hybrid," *Light* (May 1925): 16.
5. Hollis L. Townsend, *A History of Nela Park, 1911–1957* (Cleveland, Ohio: General Electric Company, n.d.), 8–15.
6. Harper Garcia Smyth, "Pageants—How Planned and Lighted," *Light* 3 (April 1925): 4–6.
7. W. C. Brown, "Your Display," *Light* 3 (October 1925): 32; Brown,

"Lighting Faults and Remedies in the Small Theatre," *Light* 3 (December 1925): 44–45.

8. Italics in original. Carl W. Maedje, "Yuletide Greetings," *Light* 4 (December 1926): 14–15, 35.

9. "The Public Takes Up Christmas Lighting," *Light* 6 (January 1928): 10.

10. C. E. Engler, "Light Sings a Christmas Carol," *Light* 5 (November 1927): 12–13, 36.

11. E. M. Watson, "Remarks on 1929 Christmas Decorations for Nela Park"; V. J. Roper, "Nela Park Christmas Lighting 1930," January 15, 1931, office record files, General Electric Company, Nela Park [hereafter NP].

12. Roper, "Nela Park Christmas Lighting 1930," NP.

13. V. J. Roper, "Proposal for 1929 Nela Christmas Lighting Displays," January 19, 1929, NP.

14. Martha J, Francis, "Behold, The Star! (An appreciation of Nela Park's Christmas display 1933)" [typescript], NP; "Nela Park's Greeting to All," *The Magazine of Light* 3 ([year end] 1933): 21.

15. H. H. Magdsick, "Pointing the Way to Prosperity Avenue," *Light* 8 (March 1930): 6–10.

16. General Electric, "Creating the Holiday Spirit," n.d., pamphlet collection, Division of Electricity, National Museum of American History; General Electric, "Suggestions for Holiday Lighting" [reprinted from *The Magazine of Light* (Fall 1935)], NP.

17. John R. Watson, "Nela Park Christmas Display 1949—The Report," 1950 [typescript]; "Nela Lights Up Tonight," *Cleveland Press*, 12 December 1941; "Holiday Lights Go On at NELA Again," *Cleveland Plain Dealer*, 10 December 1949, Nela Park clipping files, Cleveland State University Library, Cleveland Ohio.

18. "Special Christmas Preview Program 1949, WEWS Television," 1949, [typescript], NP.

19. John R. Watson, "Nela Park Christmas Display 1950" [typescript], NP.

20. Press release, "A Christmas Album," 13 December 1952, NP.

21. "Report on the 1951 Nela Park Christmas Display," NP.

22. Press release, Carl W. Maedje, "Candy Cane Lane," 12 December 1953, NP.

23. G. H. Zaar, "Christmas Lighting," *Light Magazine* 27 (October–December 1958): cover, 11–14.

24. "Market Analysis Report," 25 June 1956, NP.

25. "Annual Christmas Lighting Review," *The Magazine of Light* 20 (November 1951): 25–32.

26. Memorandum, A. C. Barr to H. L. Weiss, "Nela Park Display," February 9, 1959. NP.

27. "An Industrial Christmas," *Light Magazine* 29 (July–September 1960): 16–20.

28. Jan C. Snow, "A Little Light Work," *Avenues* (December 1993): 9.

29. Frank LaGiusa and John Sutter, "Midsummer—Halfway to Christmas," General Electric, n.d., NP.

CHAPTER FOUR

1. Albert Bliss, "The Changing Display Scene," *DW* 34 (March 1939): 5, 46.

2. Obituary, "Celebrated prop maker George Messmore Dies" [n.d.]; H. P. Preston, "From Props to Pachyderms" [typescript, n.d.], box 6, Messmore & Damon Collection, Archive Center, National Museum of American History (hereafter NMAH).

3. *The Hudson-Fulton Celebration 1909 Volume I.* (Albany, N.Y.: J.B. Lyon Company, 1910), 282–88.

4. Donald MacGregor, "Dinosaurs and Elephants to Order," *Nation's Business* (August 1925): 28–29; William Lindsay Gresham, *Monster Midway: An Uninhibited Look at the Glittering World of the Carny* (New York: Rinehart & Company, 1953), 163–68.

5. Joe Burgess, "The Rise of Papier Mache," *MR&SW* 53 (October 1923): 27–28.

6. H. P. Preston, "From Props to Pachyderms."

7. Chris Sinsabaugh, "Sparks from Detroit," 17 January 1931, M&D.

8. "The Cow," *New Yorker* 8 (11 February 1933): 12–13; "Robot Cow Moos and Gives Milk," *Popular Science Monthly* 122 (May 1935): 33.

9. Preston, "From Props to Pachyderms."

10. "A World in Miniature," *Scientific American* 143 (July 1930): 28–29, 131.

11. "It's Ballyhoo" [typescript, n.d.], box 5, M&D.

12. "Prehistoric Circus Born of Sign in Old Corktown, *Detroit News*, 28 February 1936.

13. MacGregor, "Dinosaurs and Elephants to Order," *Nation's Business* (August 1925): 28–29; "Prehistoric Mechanics," *New Yorker* 2 (25 September 1926): 17.

14. Douglas Gilbert, "It's Blue for Window Display, Red for Theatre Front, as Experts Design Ships and Beasts to Catch the Eye," *New York World-Telegram*, 8 February 1933.

15. Jo Ranson, "Coney Off to Slow Start; But with High Hopes of Getting Bonus Coin," *Variety*, 3 June 1936; "Coney Crowing as It Hits Midseason Stride After Faltering at First," *Variety*, 22 July 1936.

16. I. L. Cochrane, *Display Animation 1937: The Year Book of Motion Displays* (New York: Reeder-Morton Publications, 1937), 19.

17. Edward Thorton Heald, *The Stark County Story. Volume III. Industry Comes of Age, 1901–1917* (Canton, Ohio: Stark County Historical Society, 1952), 360–61.

18. Richard F. Dempewolff, "Santa Claus Lives in Pittsburgh," *Popular Mechanics* 92 (December 1949): 104–8, 266–70; Acker Petit, "Billion-Dollar Baby," *Pittsburgh Press*, 14 February 1965; "Gardner Displays Company," *Men and Women of Wartime Pittsburgh* (Pittsburgh, Pa.: Frank C. Harper, 1945), 352–53, Heinz History Center, Pittsburgh, Pa.

19. Albert Bliss, "Pills...Petticoats...and Plows," *DW* 44 (May 1944): 8; Thomas D. Clark, *Pills, Petticoats and Plows: The Southern Country Store* (Indianapolis, Ind.: Bobbs-Merrill Company, 1944), 141.

20. Biography, Albert Bliss, Bliss Display Corporation, October 4, 1956 [typescript], The Anna-Maria and Stephen Kellen Archives Center, Parsons The New School for Design, New York; "James Bliss Dies at 85; Ex-Window Designer," *NYT*, 14 May 1988.

21. "Window Display," *Fortune* 15 (January 1937): 91–100. Cochrane, *Display Animation 1937*, 89–93, 96, 201.

22. "Bliss in Expansion Move," *DW* 64 (March 1954): 40–41.

23. Albert Bliss, "The Changing Display Scene," *DW* 34 (March 1939): 5, 46.

24. "Lord & Taylor Windows Testify for Display," *DW* 32 (January 1938): 34; Leonard S. Marcus, *The American Store Window* (New York: Watson-Guptil, 1978), 31.

25. Albert Bliss, "The Changing Display Scene," *DW* 34 (March 1939): 5, 46.

26. "Avenue Art," *Time* 32 (5 December 1938): 37–38.

27. Editorial, "Lord & Taylor Makes Display History," *DW* 33 (December 1938): 24; "Window Display," *Fortune* 15 (January 1937): 91–100; "Motion on the Avenue," *New Yorker* 14 (7 January 1939): 14; Marcus, *The American Store Window*, 65–66; Leach, *Land of Desire*, 343–44. Lord & Taylor again entered into controversy with the Fifth Avenue

Association in 1951. See Earl Dash, "Clearer Rules on Fifth Avenue Display Sought," *Women's Wear Daily*, 29 March 1950.

28. Albert Bliss, "Display Studio Problems: III. Administration," *DW* 32 (November 1938): 8.

29. Paul Gianfagna, telephone interview, Bagni di Lucca, Italy, 1 June 2006.

30. Ad, Bliss Display Corporation, Division of Visual Merchandising, "At Last! Letters to Santa Get Results," *DW* 52 (June 1948): 28.

31. Letter, Albert Bliss to Prof. John E. Mertes, *DW* 55 (August 1949): 96–98; Albert Bliss, "Display is Store Planning," *DW* 50 (August 1947): 56, 103.

32. "Holiday Displays Attract Buyers," *NYT*, 27 June 1944, 26; ad, Bliss Display Corporation, "The Origins of Christmas Customs," *DW* 44 (March 1944): 21.

33. "NADI Votes Research Fund," *DW* 53 (July 1948): 52–53, 112; "NADI Research Committee Makes Initial Report," *DW* 53 (October 1948): 106–7; Albert Bliss, "NADI-NYU Display Research Results to be Revealed," *DW* 53 (November 1948): 44–45, 107; Bliss, "Display is Store Planning," *DW* 50 (August 1947): 56, 103.

34. Ad, Bliss Display Corporation, "Bliss Mechanical Christmas Attractions Stop Traffic!" *DW* 56 (May 1950): 23.

35. "Bliss in Expansion Move," *DW* 64 (March 1954): 40–41.

36. Albert Bliss, "Combine Emotion, Reason for Displays that Sells," *DW* 58 (May 1951): 46, 73–74; Bliss, "Without Showmanship… Display Can't Do Its Full Job," *DW* 60 (February 1952): 24, 70–72.

37. Ad, Bliss Display Corporation, "It's Christmas in Our Town," *DW* 68 (June 1956): 79.

38. Albert Bliss, "Downtown Survival," *DW* 78 (March 1961): 32, 52–53.

39. Karal Ann Marling, *Merry Christmas!*, 119.

40. Victor Gruen and Larry Smith, "The Use of Public Areas," *Shopping Towns USA: The Planning of Shopping Centers* (New York: Reinhold Publishing Corporation, 1960), 257–64; M. Jeffrey Hardwick, *Mall Maker: Victor Gruen, Architect of an American Dream* (Philadelphia: University of Pennsylvania Press, 2004), 42–43, 134–38; Sharon Zukin, *Point of Purchase: How Shopping Changed American Culture* (New York: Routledge, 2004), 257.

41. Ad, Bliss Display Corporation, "Bliss Display Salutes Freedomland," *DW* 76 (June 1960): 14–15.

42. Randall Jarrell, "A Sad Heart at the Supermarket," in *Culture for the Millions? Mass Media in Modern Society*, ed. Norman Jacobs (Princeton, N.J.: D. Van Nostrand Company, 1961), 97–110.

CHAPTER FIVE

1. Henri Schindler, *Mardi Gras: New Orleans* (New York: Flammarion, 1997), 116–23 and *Mardi Gras Treasures: Float Designs of the Golden Age* (Gretna, La.: Pelican Publishing Company, 2001); Rick Hamlin, *Tournament of Roses: A 100 Year Celebration* (New York: McGraw-Hill, 1988), 56–91; Robert Sullivan, ed., *America's Parade: A Celebration of Macy's Thanksgiving Day Parade* (New York: Time Life, Inc., 2001); Robert M. Grippo and Christopher Hoskins, *Macy's Thanksgiving Day Parade* (Charleston, S.C., Arcadia, 2004); Loran Smith, *Fifty Years on Fifty: The Orange Bowl Story* (Charlotte, N.C.: East Woods Press in Association with the Orange Bowl Committee, 1983).

2. Barr Ferree, "Elements of a Successful Parade," *Century* 60 (July 1900): 457–62; Paige W. Roberts, "'The Floral Architect': Rules and Designs for Processions," in ed. Peter Benes, *New England Celebrates: Spectacle, Commemoration, and Festivity* (Boston: Boston University Press, 2002).

3. Chicago Artificial Flower Company, "The Story of 'The Float that Jack Built,' More Truth than Poetry," 1931.

4. Rick Hamlin, *Tournament of Roses: A 100 Year Celebration* (New York: McGraw-Hill, 1988), 72–76; L. F. Vaughn, *Vaughn's Parade and Float Guide* (Minneapolis, Minn.: T. S. Denison and Company, 1956), 123; "Creating Displays for the 'Big Top,'" *DW* 61 (July 1952): 34, 57; William Tracy to Dennis Mulhearn, 10 July 1964, folder: budget 1964, Macy's Archive (hereafter Macy's); William Tracy, "How to Plan a Parade," *DW* 64 (May 1954): 54, 114–15.

5. "Flower River is a Big Parade," *Los Angeles Times*, 2 January 1909; Dana Kennedy, "Float Designer Bloomed in Each of 62 Rose Parades," *Los Angeles Times*, 26 April 1982; "Hawaiians Honor My 'Orchid Girl,'" *Pasadena Star-News*, 14 August 1960; Greg Joseph, "Isabella Coleman's Special Genius and the Rose Parade," *Pasadena Union*, 20 September 1972, biographical newspaper clipping file, Pasadena Public Library; letter to Will Downer, 28 March 1940, Coleman papers, courtesy David Coleman; interview, David Coleman, Pasadena, Calif., November 14, 2005.

6. "Details of Gay Parade," *Los Angeles Times*, 1 January 1910; "All Southern California Shares with Pasadena Triumph of Her Golden Day," *Los Angeles Times*, 2 January 1914; Jerry Doernberg, "Rose Parade Will Mark End of Work for Veteran of 55 Events," *Los Angeles Times*, 28 December 1964; Margaret Stovall, "Isabella Coleman Has Won Float Prizes for More Than 50 Years," *Pasadena Star-News*, 23 December 1965; "Top Woman Float Designer Finds Son Competitor," *Pasadena Star-News*, 29 December 1957; "Fifty Years a Champion," *Pasadena Independent*, 3 January 1954; Joseph, "Isabella Coleman's Special Genius," *Pasadena Union*, 20 September 1972; letter to Will Downer, 28 March 1940, Coleman papers; *Tournament of Roses Book* [mimeograph], "Isabella Coleman Superior Decorator Extraordinary," Pasadena Museum of History, n.d.

7. Interview, David Coleman, Pasadena, Calif., 14 November 2005.

8. "Isabella Coleman Superior Decorator Extraordinary," Pasadena Museum of History, n.d.; *Pasadena Star-News*, 31 May 1967, biographical clipping file, Pasadena Pubic Library.

9. Margaret Stovall, "Isabella Coleman Has Won Float Prizes for More than 50 Years," *Pasadena Star-News*, 23 December 1965; interview, David Coleman, Pasadena, Calif., 14 November 2005.

10. Interview, David Coleman, Pasadena, Calif., 14 November 2005; "Floats Win Right Along for 'Mrs. Rose Parade,'" *Los Angeles Times*, 2 January 1956.

11. "Busiest Grandmother Designs Rose Floats," *Los Angeles Times*, 14 December 1959.

12. "The World's Greatest Advertising Bargain at .0000523 Cent Per Person," in Edwin R. Sorver, William Dunkerly and Max Colwell, *History of the Tournament of Roses* [mimeograph], 1960, Pasadena Museum of History.

13. Interview, Bill Lofthouse, Pasadena, Calif., 14 November 2005.

14. Interview, James Offen and Johanne Offen, Fresno, Calif., 15 November 2005; Matt D. Offen, "Something New Under the Sun," *DW* 58 (March 1951): 40, 66–67; "Float Artist," *Fortnight* (24 December 1951): 14–15.

15. T. G. Wood, "Grand Lady of the Rose Parade Speaks Her Piece," Coleman papers, 1951.

16. Telephone interview, Randall Trimper, Ocean City, Md., 23 June 2003; Tracy's employment record with Ringling Brothers may be found in the employment record card file, Ringling Brothers Barnum & Bailey, Circus World Museum, Baraboo, Wisc.

17. Obituary, William T. Tracy, *Press of Atlantic City*, 24 August 1974; Tracy, "Creating Displays for the 'Big Top,'" DW 61 (July 1952): 34, 57; Tracy, "How to Plan a Parade," DW 64 (May 1954): 54, 114–15; advertisement, Ben Walters, Inc., "The Greatest Show on Earth," DW 61 (July 1952): 4; Jeanne L. Wasserman, "Fantasia Grows Outdoors," DW 78 (June 1961): 74–75, 93.
18. Contract/agreement 1 February 1955 [copy] for period 1 Feb. 1955–31 December 1960, folder: Tracy Design Co '55, Macy's.
19. Memo to Mr. Corey, 9 March 1955, folder: Tracy Design Co '55, Macy's.
20. Interview, Earl Hargrove, Landover, Md., 12 June 2002; memorandum, 18 July 1962, folder: Floats '62 (correspondence between Tracy and Dennis Mulhearn), Macy's.
21. "Newark's 'Magic' Parade," NYT, 20 November 1955; William E. Giffs, "Turkey Will Compete with Santa Tomorrow as Big Stores Parade," *Wall Street Journal*, 23 November 1955.
22. Memorandum, E. A. Hill Macy's New York Controller's office to Mrs. Corey, 9 January 1959, folder: Tracy display Co., letterhead, folder: Parade 1962 expenditures (Tracy), Macy's.
23. Interview, Manfred Bass, Mountainside, N.J., 30 April 2004.
24. *Ibid.*; Mulhearn to Hills regarding North Bergen warehouse, 23 December 1963, folder: Warehouse '63, Macy's.
25. D. Mulhearn to Thomas O. Kelly, to messrs. Dave Hill, Ed. Hill, 16 November 1964, folder: Budget '64, Macy's.
26. Interview, Manfred Bass, Mountainside, N.J., 30 April 2004.
27. Robert M. Hyatt, "The King of Floats," *American Mercury* 83 (August 1956): 93–96.
28. Vaughn, *Vaughn's Parade and Float Guide*, 52.
29. Interview, Woodrow Wilson Westberry, Earnie Seiler, and Cliff Spitzer, Miami, FL, 30 March 2005; Walter Machos, "A Year's Work for a Glance," *Miami Sunday News Magazine*, 18 December 1949, 4–5, Krake papers, Division of Politics & Reform, National Museum of American History (hereafter P&R/NMAH).
30. Interview, Cyrus Krake, Minneapolis, Minn., 25 April 2002.
31. "Cyrus Does It Again—With Electric Gulls," 1951, P&R/NMAH.
32. Telephone interview, Arva Parks, Miami, Fla, 11 March 2005.
33. "Cyrus Does It Again—With Electric Gulls" 1951, P&R/NMAH.
34. Interview, Cyrus Krake, Minneapolis, Minn., 25 April 2002.
35. Bob Murphy, "Vaughn Quits as Builder: Float King Now Sells 'Do-It-Yourself' Kits," *Minneapolis Star*, 25 December 1954, P&R/NMAH.
36. Interview, Lynn Smith, Golden Valley, Minn., 26 April 2002. A draft of Herman Smith's "memorandum agreement" for the Eisenhower parade (written on the back of a Vaughn Displays, Inc. order blank) may be found in the Smith collection, P&R/NMAH.
37. Randall Hobart, "Vaughn's Parade to Pass $1 Million," *Minneapolis Star*, 29 April 1964; Jim Klobuchar, "It's a Tinseled World," *Minneapolis Star*, 3 November 1965; Charles Whiting, "Bloomington Company Decks Out Cities to Lure Christmas Cash," *Minneapolis Star*, 18 November 1969.
38. Interview, Lynn Smith, Golden Valley, Minn., 26 April 2002.

CHAPTER SIX
1. Lancaster, *The Department Store*, 23–24 (figs 1 and 2), 26–27.
2. Allen W. Jackson, *The Half-timbered House: Its Origin, Design, Modern Plan and Construction* (New York: McBride, Nast & Company, 1912), unpaginated captions. Lee Goff, *Tudor Style: Tudor Revival Houses from 1890 to the Present* (New York: Universe, 2002), 12.
3. Arrol Gellner and Douglas Keister, *Storybook Style: America's Whimsical Homes of the Twenties* (New York: Viking, 2001), 37–38, 49–61.
4. Ad, Lord & Taylor, NYT, 4 December 1923, 12; 6 December 1923, 20.
5. 1927 Photo Album, Christmas Displays, box 127-G, John Wanamaker Collection, Historical Society of Pennsylvania [hereafter HSP].
6. Letter to Belrose Bourne, 30 March 1938, f: 6 A-B 1938, box 50, Wanamaker, HSP.
7. "Initiative and Creative Phases," notebook 1952–1954, shelf 1 box 2, Yost Collection, HSP.
8. Rocket Express monorail rides were purchased and installed in Wanamaker's Philadelphia; Kresge's Newark; the Milwaukee Boston Store; Sears State Street Chicago; Stone & Thomas, Wheeling, West Virginia; Donaldson's Minneapolis; and Leonard's Ft. Worth. "Philadelphia Children Ride Over Wanamaker's Toy Department," DW 53 (December 1948): 78; "Clint Clark Resigns Stensgaard Post," DW 55 (September 1949): 71; advertisement, "Rocket Express Systems," DW 54 (April 1949): 40 and DW 55 (November 1949): 79.
9. "'Stately and Dull Windows,'" MR&SW 78 (November 1936): 4–7; "American Display Men Say Field's Windows are Not Dull," MR&SW 78 (December 1936): 3–9; Homer Sharp, "Marshall Field's Arthur Fraser," *Visual Merchandising and Store Design* (April 1994): 16–21; Leach, *Land of Desire*, 68–70 and Leach, "Strategists of Display and the Production of Desire," in Simon J. Bronner, ed., *Consuming Visions: Accumulation and Display of Goods in America, 1880–1920* (W. W. Norton & Company, 1989), 99–132. On Fraser's Christmas display work see "Beautiful Christmas Interior Displays at Marshall Field's Retail Store," MR&SW 77 (November 1935): cover, 3–4.
10. Alice Vaneta Marker, "Display is on a Grand Scale at Marshall Field & Co." DW 53 (December 1948): 44–45, 112–13; telephone interview, Carl D. Guldager, Phoenix, Arizona, 5 July 2006.
11. Telephone interview, Sally Pozniak, Chicago, Il., 23 February 2006; Estella de Lanoi, "All the Store's a Stage at Marshall Field's," DW 50 (May 1947): 56–57; Homer Sharp, "Resume of Window Display Activities, June 1964," Marshall Field Archive, Chicago, IL.
12. Estella de Lanoi, "All the Store's a Stage at Marshall Field's," DW 50 (May 1947): 56–57.
13. Telephone interview, Sallie Pozniak, Chicago, Ill., 23 February 2006.
14. Lloyd Wendt and Herman Kogan, *Give the Lady What She Wants: The Story of Marshall Field & Company* (Chicago: Rand McNally & Company, 1952), 368. Wendt and Kogan erroneously list the years for "The Night Before Christmas" as 1946–47. The window text with photographs of the display are reproduced in Robert P. Lederman, *Christmas on State Street: 1940s and Beyond* (Chicago: Arcadia, 2002), 85–90.
15. Inez Whitely Foster, "Red Nosed Reindeer," *Christian Science Monitor*, 4 December 1948, WM10; Lederman, *Christmas on State Street*, 39–42.
16. Telephone interview, Joanna Osborne, Springfield, Mass., 23 February 2006.
17. *Ibid.*; Lederman, *Christmas on State Street*, 91–97; Marker, "Display is on a Grand Scale at Marshall Field & Co." DW 53 (December 1948): 44–45, 112–13.
18. T. H. Robsjohn-Gibbings, *Good-bye, Mr. Chippendale* (New York: Alfred A. Knopf, 1944 and 1947); ad, "Our Modern House '48 Opens Today," *Chicago Daily Tribune*, 22 September 1947; "The Modern Home of 1948," *Chicago Daily Tribune*, 29 February 1948.
19. Shirley Ware, "Chicago Becomes a Land of Make-Believe," DW 57 (December 1950): 22–23, 62; "Public Helps Set Christmas Themes in Chicago Display," DW 59 (December 1951): 28–29, 66.

EPILOGUE

1. "The Value of Tradition," *Department Store Economist* 29 (July 1966): 62–63.
2. "Christmas Ideas for windows…interiors…exteriors…Part One," *DW* 87 (September 1965): 35; "Animated—Institutional Windows," *DW* 87 (September 1965): 42–51.
3. Reinhard Hofmann to author, 28 August 2006; Edgar Williams, "Once Again, Lits Village Visits for Christmas," *Philadelphia Inquirer*, 22 November 1988; Alexis Moore, "Home for the Holidays," *Philadelphia Inquirer*, 26 November 1988; Ralph Ranalli, "Offer Warms fans of Enchanted Village," *Boston Globe*, 17 November 2003.
4. Judith Viorst, "Williamsburg Comes to Woodies Window," *Washington Post Potomac Magazine* 27 (November 1966): 17–21.
5. George K. Payne, *Creative Display* (New York: Sales Promotion Division, National Retail Merchants Association, 1965); Marling, *Merry Christmas!*, 92–94.
6. Roland Leimbach, interview, 21 November 2001.
7. Ruth Wagner, "Feline Hordes Populate Show Windows," *Washington Post*, 20 November 1960.
8. "Woodies Annual Production is Result of Two Years' Planning," *Washington Post*, 24 November 1968; Roland Leimbach, interview, Washington, D.C., 21 November 2001; "Christmas Around the World," *Washington Post*, 27 November 1962; press release, "Woodward & Lothrop's Christmas Windows, 'Colonial Williamsburg at Christmas Time,'" 23 November 1966, folder: Exhibits-Window Displays, Woodward & Lothrop Archives, Colonial Williamsburg Foundation [hereafter CWF].
9. Press release, Woodward & Lothrop's Christmas Windows "Colonial Williamsburg at Christmas," 23 November 1966. Exhibits—Window Displays—Woodward & Lothrop, CWF.
10. *Ibid.*
11. Andrew Parker to Carlisle H. Humelsine, 17 January 1967, exhibits—window displays—Woodward & Lothrop, CWF.
12. Margaret Uberman, interview, Bethesda, Md., 4 April 2004.
13. "Colonial Scenes Delight All," *Richmond Times-Dispatch*, 1 December 1969.
14. "Williamsburg Opens Windows on the Yuletide," *Panorama*, 17 December 1978, CWF.
15. Invoice, "Electrical Display Pieces," 31 August 1962, Christian Hofmann Company records.
16. Clara Baldwin, "Lit Brothers' Enchanted Colonial Village Looks Ahead to Fourth Successful Season," *DW* 87 (October 1965): 76–77, 88.
17. Gerald Lamparter, telephone interview, Philadelphia, Pa., 3 July 2006.
18. Edgar Williams, "Once Again, Lits Village Visits for Christmas," *Philadelphia Inquirer*, 22 November 1988; Moore, "Home for the Holidays;" Alviti to Bucker, 29 November 1988; petition, n.d., Office of Horticulture, Smithsonian Institution [hereafter OH/SI].
19. Moore, "Home for the Holidays."
20. Memorandum, Kathryn Meehan through Tom Freudenheim, through Peter Powers, to Robert McCormick Adams, regarding Deaccession and Disposal of "The Enchanted Village" [August 1989], OH/SI.
21. "2002 Enchanted Colonial Village at Please Touch Museum: A Meeting between Please Touch Museum and Philadelphia Foundation," Wednesday, 18 September 2002, Please Touch Museum.
22. Jane Dickinson, "Woodward & Longing: My Department Store Days in a Washington that Vanished," *Washington Post*, 30 January 1994.
23. Patricia Leigh Brown, "Savoring the Season, Window by Window," *NYT*, 20 December 1991, C1, 14.
24. Sharon Zukin, *Point of Purchase: How Shopping Changed American Culture* (New York: Routledge, 2003), 257; M. Jeffrey Hardwick, *Mall Maker: Victor Gruen, Architect of an American Dream* (Philadelphia: University of Pennsylvania Press, 2004), 2.
25. Victor Gruen and Larry Smith, *Shopping Towns, USA: The Planning of Shopping Centers* (New York: Reinhold Publishing Corporation, 1960), 257–64.
26. Paul Gianfagna, telephone interview, Bagni di Lucca, Italy, 1 June 2006.
27. Hardwick, *Mall Maker*, 217.
28. Kenneth T. Jackson, "All the World's a Mall: Reflections on the Social and Economic Consequences of the American Shopping Center," *American Historical Review* 101 (October 1996): 1111–21.

CREDITS

Cover. Copy photo, framed silhouette "greeting card," Nela Park, 1953, courtesy of the General Electric Company.

INTRODUCTION

vi. Watercolor rendering, Francis Scott Key float, ca. 1929, Messmore & Damon Collection, Division of Politics & Reform, National Museum of American History (hereafter P&R/NMAH), SI #2005-451.

2. Top left. Copy photo, "Wonderland" window by Tony Sarg, 1923, courtesy of Macy's.

2. Top right. Transparency, parade review, Seattle Seafair, ca. 1959.

2. Bottom. Copy photo, Harold G. Messmore with animated figures, ca. 1935, Messmore & Damon Collection, gift of Pam and Peter Tobiason, Archives Center, National Museum of American History (hereafter AC/NMAH).

CHAPTER ONE: DISPLAY WORLD

4. Foreground. Floral automobile, "Art & Decoration," 1914, reprinted with permission of Avery Dennison Corporation, SI #2004-62042.

4. Background. Flower templates, 1929, reprinted with permission of Avery Dennison Corporation.

6. Top left. Trimmer's tools, *A Textbook on Mercantile Decoration*, 1903, SI #2003-12961.

6. Top right. Trimmer's hands holding a bow, *A Textbook on Mercantile Decoration*, 1903, SI #2003-12960.

6. Bottom. Trimmer adjusting drape, *A Textbook on Mercantile Decoration*, 1903, SI #2005-1876.

8. Booklet cover, "Art & Decoration," 1914, reprinted with permission of Avery Dennison Corporation, SI #2004-62041.

9. Top. Trade samples, "The New Dennison Crepe," n.d., reprinted with permission of Avery Dennison Corporation, SI #2002-25509.

9. Bottom. Trade samples, Dennison crepe, n.d., reprinted with permission of Avery Dennison Corporation.

10. Top left. Booklet cover, "Gasthoff's Parade Float & Decorations," 1938.

10. Bottom left. Parade float elevations, Gasthoff, 1938.

10. Right. Booklet page, float plans, details, photo, Gasthoff, 1938.

11. Booklet cover, "Parade Floats and Decorations," Chicago Artificial Flower Co., 1930, SI #2005-25243.

12. Top. Photo, Herman Smith hanging crepe, Parker Dance Hall, Minot, N.D., 1934, Herman Smith Collection, gift of Lynn Smith, P&R/NMAH, SI #2003-20525.

12. Bottom. Photo, J&S Display truck, 1935, Herman Smith Collection, P&R/NMAH, SI #2003-20524.

14. Left. Cartoon, "Which Way Are You Taking?" *Koester School Yearbook*, ca. 1913, SI #2005-1879.

14. Right. Cover, Display Advertising shield, *Merchants Record and Show Window* 52 (May 1923), SI #2005-1877.

15. Ad, "Xmas Decoration Ideas," Harry Taylor, *Merchants Record and Show Window* 61 (August 1927): 4, SI #2002-12963.

16. Photo, Hales studio, ca. 1923, Landy R. Hales Papers, gift of Elizabeth Stuart McNulty, Lenore Hales McNulty Frey, Margaret Ann McNulty Klipp, Frances Helen McNulty Beverage, and Katharine Landa McNulty Hogben, AC/NMAH #AC0906-0000014.

17. Copy photo, Macy's 34th Street Christmas window, 1933, Hales Papers, AC/NMAH #AC0906-0000015.

18. Top left. Copy photo, Macy's 34th Street Christmas window, 1933, Hales Papers, AC/NMAH #AC0906-0000016.

18. Top right. Copy photo, Macy's 34th Street Christmas window, 1933, Hales Papers, AC/NMAH #AC0906-0000017.

18. Bottom left. Copy photo, Macy's 34th Street Christmas window, 1933, Hales Papers, AC/NMAH #AC0906-0000019.

18 Bottom right. Copy photo, Macy's 34th Street Christmas window, 1933, Hales Papers, AC/NMAH #AC0906-0000018.

19. Copy photo, Macy's 34th Street Christmas window, 1933, Hales Papers, AC/NMAH #AC0906-0000020.

CHAPTER TWO: MECHANICAL, ELECTRICAL AND EMOTIONAL EFFECTS

20. Copy photo, Fulton Street, Brooklyn, N.Y., 18 December 1968, courtesy of the *New York Times*, #806-L-17-C.

22. Trade card, Eden Musée, 1885.

23. Macy's 14th Street Christmas window, *Frank Leslie's Illustrated Newspaper*, 20 December 1884, 284, courtesy of Macy's.

24. Plate 685, Santa Claus grotto by Leonard Shogrun, *Show Window* 5 (November 1899): 220.

26. Postcard, Seigel, Cooper Co., Chicago, 1909, SI #2005-25241.

27. Top. Paper novelty toy chest, Marshall Field & Co., 1925.

27. Back cover, "Santa's Own Story Book," Kresge Department Store, Newark, N.J., ca. 1926, SI #2002-25516.

29. Photo, Wanamaker's Grand Court, 1927, John Wanamaker Collection, courtesy of the Historical Society of Pennsylvania.

CHAPTER THREE: NIGHTTIME AT NELA PARK

32. Transparency, Santa Claus leaving the North Pole, Nela Park, 1953, courtesy of Arthur Lavine.

35. Tinted photo, Nela Park entrance gate, 1927, courtesy of the General Electric Company.

36. Copy photo, illuminated ice pile, 1930, courtesy of the General Electric Company.

37. Map, traffic study, 1936, courtesy of the General Electric Company.

38. Booklet page, Suggestions for Street Decorations, reprinted from *Light Magazine*, Fall 1935, courtesy of the General Electric Company.

39. Top. Tinted photo, campus entrance and Lodge, 1936, courtesy of the General Electric Company.

39. Bottom. Brochure, "Suggestions—Ideas—Materials," 1937, courtesy of the General Electric Company.

40. Copy photo, tree construction, 1949, courtesy of the General Electric Company.

41. Tinted photo, Engineering building and illuminated trees, 1949, courtesy of the General Electric Company.

43. Magazine cover, shadowbox greeting cards, *Light Magazine* (December 1958), courtesy of the General Electric Company.

44. Collage, rendering of tree and lollipop installation, 1959, courtesy of the General Electric Company.

91. Top. Photo, tow truck float, Washington, D.C., 1948, photo by Del Ankers, courtesy of the Earl C. Hargrove Collection.

91. Bottom. Photo, live stocking models, Salem, Va., 1952, courtesy of the Earl C. Hargrove Collection.

92. Copy photo, Manfred G. Bass in Macy's Parade Studio, 25 November 1980, courtesy of the *New York Times*, #806-L-A-A-7.

93. Transparency, Hargrove, Inc. float warehouse with U. S. Bicentennial Parade floats, Landover, Maryland, 1976, photo by Mel Chamowitz, courtesy of the Earl C. Hargrove Collection.

94. Catalog centerfold, "Celebration Days," Vaughn Displays, Inc., Minneapolis, Minn., 1956, SI #2002-25549.

95. Copy photo, aerial view of the King Orange Festival Parade, ca. 1955, courtesy of the Orange Bowl Committee.

96. Copy photo, *First National Bank of Miami* float, King Orange Festival Parade, ca. 1960, courtesy of the Orange Bowl Committee.

97. Top. Rendering, Minnesota float with annotations, Vaughn Displays, King Orange Festival Parade, ca. 1955, courtesy of the Orange Bowl Committee.

97. Bottom. Rendering, Texas float, Vaughn Displays, King Orange Festival Parade, 1965, courtesy of the Orange Bowl Committee.

98. Top. Newspaper cartoon, Chuck Thorndike, *Miami Herald*, 31 December 1947, Krake Collection, P&R/NMAH, SI #2005-25246.

98. Bottom. Rendering, "Live and Play in Miami" float, ca. 1960, courtesy of the Orange Bowl Committee.

99. Top. Rendering, Southwest Bell Telephone float with annotations, ca. 1969, courtesy of the Orange Bowl Committee.

99. Bottom. Copy photo, telescoping feature, half time show, Orange Bowl, 1951, courtesy of the Orange Bowl Committee.

100. Top. Catalogue cover, Vaughn's Parade Ideas, 1958, Krake Collection, P&R/NMAH, SI #2002-25524.

100. Middle. Catalog, page 13, "automobile decorations," Vaughn's Parade Ideas, 1958, Krake Collection, P&R/NMAH, SI #2005-444.

100. Bottom. Catalog, page 25, "float designs for banks and business firms," Vaughn's Parade Ideas, 1958, Krake Collection, P&R/NMAH, SI #2005-446.

101. Top. Office 5" x 7" card file, Vaughn Displays Inc., ca. 1950-1980, Krake Collection, P&R/NMAH, SI #2006-21903.

101. Bottom. Transparency, Schenectady, N.Y., 1959.

102. Catalog cover (back), Vaughn Displays, ca. 1965, Krake Collection, P&R/NMAH.

103. Left. Catalog page, staff portraits, Vaughn Displays, Inc., Minneapolis, Minn., 1956, Krake Collection, P&R/NMAH, SI #2002-25525.

103. Right. Catalog page, float decorating materials, Vaughn Displays, Inc., Minneapolis, Minn., 1956, Krake Collection, P&R/NMAH, SI #2002-25546.

105. Copy photo, "Why Daddy Saves" float, First Dakota National Banks, Fargo, N.D., Centennial of Fargo, 1950, Smith Collection, P&R/NMAH, SI #2003-20529.

CHAPTER SIX: TUDOR TOWN TO TRACT HOME

106. Copy photo, Cozy Cloud Cottage, 1948, courtesy of Macy's.

108. Top left. Rendering, toy department display bridge, n.d., Hales Collection, AC/NMAH, #AC0906-0000012.

108. Top right. Rendering, toy department display drawbridge, n.d., Hales Collection, AC/NMAH, #AC0906-0000010.

108. Bottom left. Rendering, toy department display tower, n.d., Hales Collection, AC/NMAH, #AC0906-0000013.

108. Bottom right. Rendering, toy department display house, n.d., Hales Collection, AC/NMAH, #AC0906-0000011.

109. Copy photo, *Macy's Wonderland Village* tableau, ca. 1927, Hales Collection, AC/NMAH, #AC0906-0000022.

110. Copy photo, Macy's toy department, 1927, Hales Collection, AC/NMAH, #AC0906-0000021.

111. Left. Children's souvenir, Macy's Wonderland, 1927, Hales Collection, AC/NMAH, #AC0906-0000002.

111. Right. Poster study, Macy's Wonderland, 1927, Hales Collection, AC/NMAH, #AC0906-0000006.

112. Poster, *A Wonderful Trip by Radio Ship* stage show, 1926, John Wanamaker Collection, courtesy of the Historical Society of Pennsylvania.

113. Photo, Santa with children and prop ledgers, Philadelphia, 1926, John Wanamaker Collection, courtesy of the Historical Society of Pennsylvania.

114. Left. Booklet, *Thro' Venture Village*, Wanamaker's, Philadelphia, 1928, SI #2004-62040.

114. Right. Photostat, *On Candy Stick Lane in the Land of Make-Believe*, John Wanamaker Collection, courtesy of the Historical Society of Pennsylvania.

115. Photo, construction of Candy Stick Lane, Wanamaker's, Philadelphia, 1926, John Wanamaker Collection, courtesy of the Historical Society of Pennsylvania.

116. Photo, entrance, *The Land of Really-So*, 1931, John Wanamaker Collection, courtesy of the Historical Society of Pennsylvania.

118. Copy photo, toy window display, ca. 1951, courtesy of Macy's.

119. Copy photo, Marshall Field main aisle, ca. 1956, courtesy of Macy's.

120. Booklet cover, "Rudolph the Red-Nosed Reindeer," 1939.

121. Copy photo, reindeer relaxing in kitchen, *Cozy Cloud Cottage*, 1948, courtesy of Macy's.

122. Floor plan for the living room of the *Cozy Cloud Cottage* 1948, courtesy of Macy's.

123. Copy photo, Santa Claus setting with annotations, *Cozy Cloud Cottage*, 1948, courtesy of Macy's.

124. Copy photo, penguin drive-in and snack bar, *Cozy Cloud Cottage*, ca. 1950, courtesy of Macy's.

125. Copy photo, spinning display elements, approach to *Cozy Cloud Cottage*, ca. 1972, courtesy of Macy's.

EPILOGUE: WHERE THE STORES WERE

126. Digital photo, restoration of animated figures, 2002, courtesy of the Please Touch Museum.

128. Illustration, George K Payne, *Display World 74* (July 1959): 52.

129. Magazine page, animated Three Bears window display, Woodward & Lothrop, *Collier's* (22 December 1951): 29.

130. Top. Copy photo, animated Governor's Palace window display, Woodward & Lothrop, 1966, courtesy of the Colonial Williamsburg Foundation.

130. Bottom. Copy photo, animated Wythe house parlor and staircase window display, Woodward & Lothrop, 1966, courtesy of the Colonial Williamsburg Foundation.

131. Copy photo, animated wig shop window display, Woodward &

Lothrop, 1966, courtesy of the Colonial Williamsburg Foundation.

132. Cover, "Lit Brothers Enchanted Christmas Village," Philadelphia, Pa., 1963, SI #2005-4662.

133. Top left. Transparency, entrance to Lit Brothers' Enchanted Christmas Village, 1966, courtesy of Gerald Lamparter.

133. Top right. Transparency, schoolroom, Lit Brothers' Enchanted Christmas Village, 1966, courtesy of Gerald Lamparter.

133. Bottom left. Transparency, blacksmith, Lit Brothers' Enchanted Christmas Village, 1966, courtesy of Gerald Lamparter.

133. Bottom right. Transparency, three-quarter-scale figures, Lit Brothers' Enchanted Christmas Village, 1966, courtesy of Gerald Lamparter.

137. Top. Transparency, *Our Favorite Book* float, Tournament of Roses, 1954.

137. Bottom. Copy photo, Doo Dah parade, Pasadena, 3 January 1981, courtesy of the *New York Times*, #5835-L.

138. Top left. Trade catalog, "Christmas Decorations for Shopping Centers" (1970), 31, courtesy of the Valley Decorating Co.

138. Top right. Trade catalog, "Christmas Decorations for Shopping Centers" (1970), p. 49, courtesy of the Valley Decorating Co.

138. Bottom. Copy photo, Joan Benjamin of Spaeth Design preparing mechanical figures for Lord & Taylor, 24 November 1984, courtesy of the New York Times, #806-L-17-C.

140. Copy photo, Roundtable forum for Santa Clauses, 11 October 1948, courtesy of the New York Times, 5041L.

ACKNOWLEDGMENTS

I wish to thank the people and institutions whose collections, memories, and kindnesses shaped this book. I owe a special debt to the creative individuals in the display business, and their families, who donated primary source material to the National Museum of American History. Pam Tobiason gave her father's Messmore & Damon Company papers; the late Cyrus Krake gave photographs and his parade float file; Lynn Smith gave his father's display scrapbooks; and Elizabeth Stuart McNulty, Lenore Hales McNulty Frey, Margaret Ann McNulty Klipp, Frances Helen McNulty Beverage, and Katharine Landa McNulty Hogben, gave the Landy R. Hales papers.

Many individuals generously shared their collections and reminiscences in interviews. Earl C. Hargrove opened his company's photo archive, and entertained with a tour of *American Celebration on Parade*, his collection of floats and animated holiday displays exhibited at Shenandoah Caverns, Virginia. Roland Leimbach treated me to a first-person account of the development of Woodward & Lothrop's *Christmas in Colonial Williamsburg* windows. Margaret Uberman graciously allowed me to interview her about the history of Washington, D.C.'s National Wax Museum and the Williamsburg National Wax Museum. Woodrow Wilson Westberry, Earnie E. Seiler, and Cliff Spitzer, Jr., discussed the Vaughn Display Company and Miami's King Orange Festival, along with Arva Moore Parks and Russell Etling, who kindly let me review the Orange Bowl Committee's vast trove of photographs and float renderings. Bill Lofthouse discussed the history of the Tournament of Roses, and shared several examples of float renderings made for Isabella Coleman. David Coleman shared his mother's scrapbooks with me, and offered key insights about her working methods as a float builder. Adria DeBaca and Nicole O'Neil of the Tournament of Roses Committee indulged my requests for parade float images, as did Dan McLaughlin of the Pasadena Public Library, and Julie Stiles, Steve Tice, and Kirk Myers of the Pasadena Museum of History, in whose reading room Ann Scheid made timely suggestions and introductions. Georgen Gilliam of the Nantucket Historical Society and George Korn shared their knowledge of Tony Sarg. Marni Artzner-Wolf of the McKinley Museum and National Memorial traced the history of the Old King Cole Company for me. Ted Hathaway of the Minneapolis Public Library compiled business records relating to the Vaughn Company. Jay Emery of New Orleans's Bergeron Studio & Gallery shared photographs of city department store displays. Reinhard Hofmann of Germany's Christian Hofmann Company responded to my queries for business records and photographs documenting the development of animated figures and Enchanted Villages for American department stores.

Manfred G. Bass shared his insight into the business of William T. Tracy and Macy's Thanksgiving Day Parade, supported in depth by Macy's Robin Hall, Bob Rutan, Scott Byers, and Edward Jay Goldberg, whose generosity allowed me to have an extended stay in the store's archive, and a tour of Macy's Parade Float Studio. James

Offen and Johanne Offen shared scrapbooks and a reminiscence written by Valley Decorating Company founder Matt Offen. Valerie Ann Baum Lingeman shared float renderings and a privately printed reminiscence about the life of artist Louis Kennel.

At Philadelphia's Please Touch Museum, Nancy Kolb, John T. McDevitt, Tom Becket, Chris Hillman, Jason Smereczynski, and Stacey A. Swigart provided photographs and a close inspection of their Enchanted Colonial Village. Tony Jahn opened the Marshall Field Archive and helped arrange telephone interviews with long-time Field employees JoAnna Osborne, JoAnn Sharp, Sally Pozniak, and Carl D. Guldager. At General Electric, Kathy Presciano kindly shared Nela Park's compelling collection of outdoor holiday lighting photographs, slides, and display elements, many of which are used to this day. Frank LaGiusa graciously entertained me with an interview about his career as a lighting engineer and designer. Paul Gianfagna reminisced about his and his father John Gianfagna's studio work for Bliss Display, and arranged for the photography of his studio drawings. Gerald Lamparter shared reminiscences and the superb color slides that he took as a youth of Lit Brothers' Enchanted Christmas Village.

I am also indebted to the kindnesses of Richard Price of the Heinz History Center; Susan Pearl of the Prince Georges County, Maryland Historical Society; X. Theodore Barber of the New School; Janet Bunde of the New York University Archives; Christie Lutz of the Seely G. Mudd Manuscript Library, Princeton University; William C. Barrow of the Cleveland State University Library; David Shackelford and Sarah Davis of the B & O Railroad Museum; Barbara Mathe of the American Museum of Natural History; Erin Foley of the Circus World Museum; Molly Rawls of the Forsyth County Public Library, Winston-Salem, North Carolina; Amanda Lett of the Tulsa Historical Society; Kerry McLaughlin and Robert A. Friedman of the Historical Society of Pennsylvania; Glenda Kitto and Kimberly True of the Avery Dennison Corporation; Phyllis Collazo of the *New York Times* Photo Archive; Jennifer Perilli of the *Richmond Times-Dispatch* Library; Richard Hourahan of the Rye, New York Historical Society; Playland historian Nina Cohen; Ron Giordano of the H.S. Crocker Co.; Angel Daniels of Morey's Pier; the late Charles F. Cummings of the Newark Public Library; David Angerhofer of the Maryland Historical Society; Chris Hunter of the Schenectady Museum; Laura Finkel of Vassar College Libraries Special Collections; and Charles Driscoll, Catherine Grosfils, Donna Cooke, Marianne Martin, and Cary Carson of the Colonial Williamsburg Foundation.

David Spaeth and Sandy Spaeth entertained me at length in their New York design studio and shared reminiscences about their company's display work. Thomas D. Rebbie of Philadelphia Toboggan Coaster shared his extensive photograph collection documenting the history of the amusement industry and its relationship to display. Arthur Lavine generously made his exquisite photographs of 1950s holiday lighting installations available to me for the asking. Martin M. Pegler shared his working knowledge of the display business with me, and entertained with his voluminous collection of still photographs. Barry Laudau pointed me in the direction of a collection of historic display photographs that added immeasurably to the Museum's holdings on the subject. I also benefited from talks with Marvin Bond, Jamie Becker, Amy Meadows, Robert Dorfman, Randall Trimper, Sal Lenzo, Marilu Menendez, Rick Walsh, Stu Widdes, John Gantert, Jack Barkla, B. J. Bendyna, Dominic Festa, Karen Jolis, Joe Rotundo, Polly Flossum, Dennis Flaherty, Carol Clarke, Aura Levitas, Jeff Winsper, Mel Chamowitz, and Moffat Welsh.

I wish to thank my Smithsonian and National Museum of American History colleagues, without whose kind consideration and encouragement this project would not have been possible. In the Division of Politics and Reform: Harry R. Rubenstein, Lisa Kathleen Graddy, Barbara Clark Smith, Harry Rand, Marilyn Higgins, Deborah Hashim, Patricia Mansfield, Sarah Murphy, Keith E. Melder, Edith P. Mayo, Jason Usher, Kelly Warnick, and Jessica Csoma; the National Museum of American History Archives Center: Craig Orr, John Flecker, Deborrah Richardson, Vanessa Broussard, Rueben Jackson, Catherine Keen, Susan Strange, Allison Oswald, and Kay Peterson. The National Museum of American History Branch Library: Chris Cotrill, Jim Roan, Stephanie Thomas, Mike Hardy, and the late Helen Holley; Cooper-Hewitt National Design Museum Library: Steven Van Dyke; Dibner Library of the History of Science and Technology: Kirsten van der Veen; Smithsonian Institution Archives: Robert Johnstone and Ellen Alers; Smithsonian Photographic Services: Joe Goulait, Joyce Goulait, Larry Gates, Jeff Tinsley, Hugh Talman, Richard Strauss, John Dolliver, David Burgevin, and Carl Hansen. I also wish to thank museum friends and colleagues Susan Myers, Priscilla Wood, Valeska Hilbig, Nigel Briggs, Katherine Campbell, Russell Cashdollar, Dana Greil, Matt MacArthur, Arthur P. Molella, Carlene Stephens, Maggie Dennis, Gretchen Jennings, David Haberstich, Helena Wright, Peter Liebhold, Ellen Dorn, Bill Tabor, Amy Levin, Anne Marie Halsey, Leslie Overstreet, Amy Henderson, Marc Pachter, Jim Gardner, Melinda Machado, Dennis S. Dickinson, and Brent D. Glass.

For their kind advice and criticism I wish to thank Rosemary Regan, who edited and commented upon a first draft of the manuscript, and for the criticism and insights of Charles F. McGovern, James J. Kimble, Robert W. Rydell, and Karal Ann Marling.

At Princeton Architectural Press I wish to thank designer Sara Stemen and editor Jennifer N. Thompson for their cool-hunter eyes and passion for magical books.

WLB
Washington, D.C.